When I once lost a political race, my preacher brother-in-law said it might be a "reverse calling." In that same spirit, the remarkable Barry Black has written a book that turns losses into wins. His storytelling and his devotion to Scripture create a captivating guide for anyone facing adversity, which is all of us.

LAMAR ALEXANDER
U.S. Senator (Tennessee)

The truth in this book comes with a capital *T*, and it will nourish and strengthen your soul. If you are serious about your faith, you will benefit from reading *The Blessing of Adversity*.

MARK PRYOR
U.S. Senator (Arkansas)

From growing up in a public housing project in Baltimore to counseling U.S. senators in the marble halls of Washington, Chaplain Black has truly lived and witnessed the blessings of adversity. In this book, he offers a compelling and uniquely American perspective on the power of faith and the resilience of the human spirit.

AMY KLOBUCHAR
U.S. Senator (Minnesota)

Barry Black is my counselor, my mentor, and my friend. His wisdom is built on life experiences and grounded in faith. *The Blessing of Adversity* is a guide to draw purpose from life's troubles and strength from God's Word. It is not just a book to read, but a roadmap to keep with you through life.

JOHNNY ISAKSON
U.S. Senator (Georgia)

Chaplain Black has written a book that answers the question, "Why me, God?" More importantly, it is a detailed guidebook on how to turn adversity into a positive.

MICHAEL ENZI
U.S. Senator (Wyoming)

THE
Blessing
OF
Adversity

*Finding your God-given purpose
in life's troubles*

BARRY C. BLACK

TYNDALE HOUSE PUBLISHERS, INC.
CAROL STREAM, ILLINOIS

Library of Congress Cataloging-in-Publication Data

Black, Barry C.
  The blessing of adversity : finding your God-given purpose in life's troubles / Barry C. Black.
    p. cm.
  Includes bibliographical references.
  ISBN 978-1-4143-4845-2 (hc) — ISBN 978-1-4143-2680-1 (sc)   1. Suffering—Religious aspects—Christianity.   I. Title.
  BV4909.B53 2011
  248.8'6—dc22   2010046172

To Dr. Frank W. Hale, Jr.,

who taught me that

faithfulness is more important

than success

Contents

Introduction

MOST PEOPLE SEE TROUBLE AS SOMETHING NEGATIVE and try to avoid it whenever possible. But I'm convinced that if we learn to greet our troubles with joy, we can turn our adversity into advantage and find God's purpose in our lives. That's right. If you learn to see God's blessing in adversity, you'll come to understand what King David meant when he wrote, "It is good for me that I was afflicted" (Psalm 119:71, ESV).

Maybe you've just gone through a painful divorce. You feel devastated and alone. Will you waste your pain, or will you permit God to use it for His glory? Or maybe you've just discovered that one of your children is addicted to cocaine. Can God bring any good out of your predicament? Can He enable you to overcome your season of distress? Perhaps you're facing a health challenge, or you've just been fired from your job. How do you deal with life's valleys? If "God is working for the good of those who love Him" (Romans 8:28), is He not also able to empower you to find His blessings in your troubles?

Everyone goes through seasons of difficulty. Sometimes the challenge is financial, such as when the money doesn't stretch to the end of the month, or we're forced to lose a home to foreclosure, or we find ourselves suddenly unemployed. At other times the difficulty comes as wrenching grief, when what we once felt certain we would always have—family, joy, peace—is irretrievably lost in the midst of painful circumstances.

The Blessing of Adversity provides a blueprint for finding peace in the midst of tough times. If you are wrestling with life's trials, it will empower you to embrace your challenges and acknowledge the inevitability of trouble. For "all who live godly lives will suffer persecution" (2 Timothy 3:12). In the pages that follow, you will learn how to deal with God's seasons of silence, how to encourage yourself in life's storms, and how to find God's blessings in adversity.

Furthermore, you'll learn how to use your pain to bless others. Who better to offer comfort and understanding in times of trial or grief than someone who has already been through a similar experience? When you're suffering, would you rather talk to someone who can speak only theoretically about your pain or to someone who has already walked a mile in your shoes? In the same way, you can share with others the comfort you have received from God during your own tough times.

The Blessing of Adversity is designed to be a user-friendly guide for dealing with life's storms. It distills the wisdom I have gained from thirty years of pastoral counseling, and from doctorates in theology and psychology, and develops it into a practical plan of action that will help you find your God-given purpose in life's troubles.

Let's begin our journey.

PART I

Mastering the Basics

I

CELEBRATE YOUR TROUBLES

HAVE YOU EVER LOOKED BACK at one of the difficult seasons of your life and seen more positives than negatives? Have you ever said hooray for your troubles? King David did. He said, "Before I was afflicted I went astray, but now I obey your word" (Psalm 119:67, NIV). In other words, he found the blessing in his adversity.

If you've ever celebrated your troubles, you've followed the guidance given by the apostle James: "Consider it pure joy, my brothers, whenever you face trials of many kinds, because you know that the testing of your faith develops perseverance. Perseverance must finish its work so that you may be mature and complete, not lacking anything" (James 1:2-4, NIV).

Isn't that an amazing statement? "Consider it pure joy when you face trials." In other words, greet your trials and tribulations as friends and allies, companions who will help to develop your maturity, preparing you to fulfill your God-given purpose for living.

One of my neighbors has wind chimes on his back patio. When a storm is imminent and the wind begins to kick up, I enjoy listening to the beautiful music of those chimes. And just as those chimes make music in the midst of a storm, so we should make music with our lives in the midst of our troubles. When you are facing your greatest troubles, there are six things you can do to help you celebrate your troubles: *guard your tongue, stay positive, be constant, grow up, use your map,* and *control your doubts.*

Guard Your Tongue

It's so easy to bemoan our predicaments. In the words of the old spiritual, we want to cry out, "Nobody knows the trouble I've seen." Jacob had this experience. For thirteen years, he thought that his beloved son Joseph was dead. Lamenting his terrible plight, he cried out, "All these things are against me!" (Genesis 42:36, NKJV).

The problem with bemoaning our troubles is that we can begin to speak self-fulfilling prophecies, convincing ourselves that our anxiety-laden statements must come true. Proverbs 18:21 says, "The tongue has the power of life and death" (NIV). The words you speak—to yourself and others—can bring good or ill, healing or hurt. So think about whatever is true, noble, right, pure, lovely, admirable, excellent, and praiseworthy (Philippians 4:8, NIV), and lay the foundation for wholesome and edifying speech.

Stay Positive

Learning to celebrate our troubles begins when we view trouble as a positive force in our lives. Winston Churchill said, "A pessimist sees the difficulty in every opportunity; an optimist sees the opportunity in every difficulty." Do you see opportunities in your difficulties? No matter what you're going through, strive to discover something positive.

The apostle Paul probably wrote his letter to the Philippians while imprisoned in Rome. But instead of complaining about his plight, Paul points to the opportunities he found in his difficult circumstances: "What has happened to me has really served to advance the gospel. As a result, it has become clear throughout the whole palace guard and to everyone else that I am in chains for Christ" (Philippians 1:12-13, NIV). Isn't that fantastic? Paul saw his imprisonment and impending martyrdom as a means to advance the gospel. Talk about accentuating the positive! Paul is an amazing example of optimism.

How about you? Do you see your troubles positively? You can be like Paul and his fellow missionary Silas, who prayed and sang hymns to God when they were imprisoned. You can highlight the positive by remembering that "in everything God is working for the good of those who love Him" (Romans 8:28).

One of my minister friends visited a hospitalized church member whose leg had been amputated. He struggled to think of something positive to say to her, but drew a blank. As he sat in the woman's hospital room waiting for inspiration, she broke the silence with a startling statement: "Pastor, thank God it's as good as it is. I could've lost both legs." Her positive outlook and optimistic words inspired my friend to more conscientiously seek to find life's positives and look for blessings in his adversity.

Be Constant

When you think and speak positively about your troubles, refusing to complain about your fate, you produce constancy or steadfastness. The Greek word is *hupomone*, which reflects the constancy Paul writes about in Galatians 6:9: "Don't become weary in doing good, for in due season you will reap a harvest if you don't lose heart." It was the attribute that nineteenth-century British prime minister Benjamin Disraeli emphasized when he said, "The secret of success is constancy of purpose."

King David succeeded because of constancy of purpose. The account of his anointing as king is recorded in 1 Samuel 16, but he didn't become king until some fifteen years later (2 Samuel 5). During the intervening period, he was relentlessly pursued by the most powerful man in Israel at the time, King Saul. But David didn't give up. He persevered. And from his troubles he produced memorable poetry and music, which make up much of the book of Psalms.

What success have you forfeited because you lacked constancy of purpose? Think of the thousands each year who pursue academic degrees but who give up when it gets difficult and fail to complete the program. Or think of the millions who begin a diet but falter before they achieve their goals. Those who learn to celebrate their troubles will produce constancy from their hardships and overcome their tough times.

Time and again, I've seen people with ordinary talents possess a constancy of purpose that enabled them to achieve far more than their more gifted colleagues. They plod along patiently, like the tortoise racing the hare in *Aesop's Fables*, and with steady perseverance surmount every obstacle and win the race.

Grow Up

Saying hooray for your troubles can also help you grow up. The apostle Paul declares, "When I grew up, I put away childish things" (1 Corinthians 13:11, NLT). This is what James is talking about when he says, "Perseverance must finish its work so that you may be mature and complete, not lacking anything" (James 1:4, NIV).

Nearly everyone has rough edges that need to be smoothed on the journey toward maturity. We all need to put away childish things—and trouble may be just the prompting we need. Joseph's brothers were transformed by hardships, and so was Joseph himself (Genesis 42 and 50). They all became more gracious and caring after enduring some of life's trials and uncertainty, pain and setbacks.

I had a friend in the military who reminded me of Joseph's brothers. This man had many rough edges. He spoke impulsively, refused to be punctual, missed deadlines, and struggled with grammar. As the years flew by, we'd see each other from time to time and interact. With the passing of time, I saw positive changes in this man. He began speaking with judicious forethought, embracing punctuality, meeting deadlines, and using correct grammar. He talked to me about the hard work required to bring about these improvements. He had put away childish things and developed maturity.

Are you moving in the direction of maturity? Eleanor Roosevelt provided a guide for measuring our maturity: "A mature person is one who does not think only in absolutes, who is able to be objective even when deeply stirred emotionally, who has learned that there is both good and bad in all people and all things, and who walks humbly and deals charitably with the circumstances of life."[1] That's a worthy destination, isn't it?

Use Your Map

Like most journeys of any great length, it's easier to get where we're going if we have a map. What map do we need to reach the destination of maturity? We need the map of God's wisdom. James talks about this map in the context of his discussion about rejoicing during tough times. He writes, "If any of you lacks wisdom, he should ask God, who gives generously to all without finding fault, and it will be given to him. But when he asks, he must believe and not doubt, because he who doubts is like a wave of the sea, blown and tossed by the wind" (James 1:5-6, NIV).

Solomon sought such wisdom. At the beginning of his reign, he asked God to give him the ability to discern right from wrong, the requisite wisdom to guide the Israelites. God was pleased to grant his request (1 Kings 3). Solomon could have asked for many other things—long life, victory over his enemies, or great wealth. He didn't. He simply asked for wisdom, believing it was the key to everything else he needed.

We, too, need such wisdom. Plato said, "Wise men speak because they have something to say, fools because they have to say something." How often have we spoken when we should have kept silent, and kept silent when we should have spoken? God's wisdom is like a GPS, guiding us through the twists and turns of life. In order to find God's purpose in life's troubles, we must request wisdom from our generous God.

Seeking God's wisdom shows humility and honors God. We're basically confessing, "Lord, I'm not smart enough to know which road to take without Your guidance and providence. I need You to show me what to do." Why wouldn't God move heaven and earth to honor such a petition?

Control Your Doubts

God's wisdom comes at the price of controlling your doubts. James reminds us that those who doubt will receive nothing from God (James 1:6-7). Don't miss the blessing of wisdom because of doubt.

In Mark 9:14-24 we find the story of a father who asked Jesus to heal his demon-possessed son. But the father expressed doubts that disappointed Jesus. When he saw Jesus' disappointment, the father said, "I do believe; help me overcome my unbelief!" (Mark 9:24, NIV).

Like that distressed father, our doubts are sometimes complicated and nuanced, hindering our faith. Belief and unbelief are engaged in a civil war within our hearts. C. S. Lewis once described how complicated our doubts can be. He said, "We're not necessarily doubting that God will do the best for us: we are wondering how painful the best will turn out to be."[2] By conquering our doubts when facing our troubles, we prepare ourselves for God's best work in our lives.

AN ACTION PLAN TO HELP YOU CELEBRATE YOUR TROUBLES

> *Guard your tongue.*

> *Stay positive.*

> *Be constant.*

> *Grow up.*

> *Use your map.*

> *Control your doubts.*

2

TRUST GOD'S PLAN

MY MOTHER CAME HOME from her job as a maid one day with a bag in her hand. My siblings and I surrounded her, anticipating that she would reveal some goodies. The first thing she pulled out was a thick, old record album. Leaving my siblings to discover the other treasures, I grabbed the album and ran to our little record player to see what music would delight my eight-year-old ears. Instead of music, however, I discovered two melodious sermons by Peter Marshall, who was chaplain of the U.S. Senate from 1947 to 1949.

At that time, not only did I not know who Peter Marshall was, I also didn't know the Senate had a chaplain. One thing I did know: Marshall's lyrical language mesmerized me. I played the recording so many times that it became scratchy. Having memorized those sermons, I recited entire paragraphs for my inner-city friends, who enjoyed my imitation of Marshall's Scottish accent. I never dreamed I would one day stand where Peter Marshall stood, as the sixty-second chaplain of the U.S. Senate. But God had a plan for my life, and He gave me an early glimpse.

God has a plan for every life. He opens doors that no human can shut. Those who would learn to celebrate their troubles must learn to trust God's providence, sovereignty, and plans. They must accept God's plan for their lives, even if the road leads through a garden of Gethsemane or a mountain called Calvary.

Just as surely as God has a plan for individuals, He has a plan for nations. He had a plan for Israel even when they were in Babylonian captivity (Jeremiah 29). While God's people languished far from home, He spoke through the words of the prophet Jeremiah, telling them to plant gardens, build houses, get married, have children, and pray for the prosperity of their captors (Jeremiah 29:5-7). God then revealed His plan to prosper Israel, to give them a future and hope, and to bring them to a desired destination (Jeremiah 29:11-13). He promised that they'd one day be delivered from their captivity.

That same God wants to help us celebrate our troubles and overcome our tough times. He has a plan for every life, a plan designed to bring us to a desired destination.

Surrender to God's Providence

Israel, in captivity, had to learn how to trust and surrender to God's providence. Despite what several false prophets predicted, they would not spend only a brief time in Babylon. They would be captives there for *seventy years* (Jeremiah 29:10). Therefore, God instructed them to plant trees, build houses, get married, and nurture their children.

Eli the priest learned to submit to God's providence through the negative consequences of his failure to discipline his sons. When God revealed His judgment through young Samuel the prophet, Eli responded to the terrible news with these words: "He is the Lord. May He do what He thinks best" (1 Samuel 3:18). In other words, he humbly submitted to God's loving, but painful, providence.

It's easier to accept God's providence when we remember that He really desires to bless us. As Oscar Wilde observed, "What seems to us as bitter trials are often blessings in disguise." Trusting God's sovereignty and wisdom can empower us to find goodness even in suffering and setbacks.

Believe in God's Kindness

It's easier to surrender to God's providence when you already believe in His kindness. Captive Israel was told that God was thinking about them and that He lovingly desired that they would experience His best (Jeremiah 29:11-12). God isn't your enemy; He's your friend. He's rooting for you. "'As surely as I live,' declares the Lord God, 'I take no pleasure in the destruction of the wicked, but that the wicked turn from their ways and live. Turn, turn, for why will you die, O house of Israel?'" (Ezekiel 33:11). God wants to save, not destroy.

David knew about God's paternal kindness. He writes, "I was young and now I am old, yet I have never seen the righteous forsaken or their children begging bread" (Psalm 37:25, NIV). Do you have that kind of confidence in God's power and love? Have you ever seen the righteous forsaken?

When I was in eighth grade, I came home from school one day to discover my family's furniture outside on the sidewalk. Our landlord had evicted us for failing to pay rent. The future seemed bleak. In spite of the dark clouds that loomed on our financial horizon, I didn't feel much anxiety because I trusted my mother. I knew her maternal kindness and love would find a way to keep a roof over our heads, that she'd somehow find opportunities in our adversity.

Similarly, our gracious heavenly Father, who loves us with incomprehensible affection, will look out for our best interests. As Psalm 31:15 suggests, our times are in His hands. Jesus said, "If God so clothes the grass of the field, which today is alive and tomorrow is thrown into the oven, will he not much more clothe you, O you of little faith?" (Matthew 6:30, ESV).

Have your anxieties prompted you to doubt God's fatherly love? Be encouraged. He loved you enough to die for your salvation, providing heaven's choicest gift, His Son. If He didn't withhold His only Son from us, is there anything we need that He won't supply?

Accept God's Chastisement

Though we can rejoice in God's paternal kindness, we must be prepared to receive His chastisement, as well. Good parents punish their children in love. In Revelation 3:19, the risen Christ says, "Those whom I love I discipline." Israel's Babylonian captivity was a part of God's discipline, and the people needed to accept it as correction from someone who cared about them.

After David's adultery with Bathsheba, God warned him that the baby Bathsheba had conceived would die (2 Samuel 12:14). David fasted and prayed, but the baby still died (2 Samuel 12:14-23). When David learned of the child's death, he got up, bathed, and ate. His servants were surprised by how calmly David seemed to accept the baby's death. Then David said, "While the child was alive, I fasted and prayed, thinking perhaps God might change His mind. But the child is dead now, and nothing can bring him back. I surrender to God's will" (2 Samuel 12:22-23).

Have you learned to accept discipline from God? Can you

receive a celestial spanking with the knowledge that God's love is what prompts Him to punish you?

Live with Hope

How hopeful are you? Captive Israel was told that God wanted to give them a future and a hope (Jeremiah 29:11). He wants to do the same for you. This should enable you to live with hope, to encounter your troubles believing that right will eventually win. In fact, the Bible says that you are "saved by hope" (Romans 8:24, KJV).

Hope enables you to keep your sanity during the worst times. David cried, "I would have fainted had I not believed that I would see the goodness of the Lord in the land of the living" (Psalm 27:13). Do you believe that God's purposes prevail? If so, you're living with hope.

The poet Emily Dickinson correctly observed, "Hope is the thing with feathers that perches in the soul, and sings the tune without the words and never stops at all." Those who live with hope will have a tune, even when no lyrics exist, trusting God even when they don't understand what He's doing.

Believe God's Revelation over Human Speculation

Israel in captivity heard the speculations of false prophets (Jeremiah 29:8-9). Their time of trouble was made more difficult by those who professed to speak for God but didn't. These false seers predicted that Israel's exile would be brief, contradicting God's words through His true prophet, Jeremiah, who challenged the people to believe God's words.

As you face life's challenges, many so-called experts will write prescriptions to guarantee your success. Some will tell you to pursue wealth and status, while others will suggest that real joy is experienced by finding the right relationships. Still others will recommend a disbelief in the supernatural so that you won't feel inhibited when you do what comes naturally. Don't walk in the counsel of the ungodly (Psalm 1:1), but instead look to God's Word for guidance.

In 1 Kings 13, we find the story of a true prophet who was sent to the northern kingdom of Israel to condemn King Jeroboam's idolatry. God told this prophet not to eat with anyone, but to return home immediately. A false prophet, however, convinced the true prophet that God had given a different message and that the true prophet should come home and fellowship with the false prophet. The true prophet disobeyed God's directive, which God had spoken directly to him, saying yes instead to the false prophet's request. As a result, God spoke to the false prophet with a message of judgment about the true prophet. This story helps us to see the importance of believing God's words over earthly voices.

To whom do you listen? From where do you receive your guidance and inspiration? Embrace the sacred Scriptures that can make you wise unto salvation. "Let God be true and everyone else a liar" (Romans 3:4).

Seek God with Intensity

God told the Israelites, who were in Babylonian captivity, how to overcome their predicament: "You will seek me and find me when you seek me with all your heart" (Jeremiah 29:13, NIV). Intensity matters. James 5:16 emphasizes this: "The earnest, fervent prayer of the righteous avails much." In Matthew 7:7, God promises His people, "Keep on seeking, and you will find" (NLT). As you go through the valley of trouble, seek God with intensity.

John Keats once opined, "The excellence of every art is its intensity, capable of making all disagreeables evaporate." As you face the disagreeable winds of trouble, your intensity in seeking God can make them evaporate.

Stay Productive

The captive Israelites were admonished to stay productive, and indeed they did. They were told to plant and build, marry and parent. Many, like Daniel and his three friends, flourished in captivity, becoming governmental leaders whose prophetic utterances preserved their nation. God wants us to be productive, even during our tough times. His first command to humanity was "be fruitful" (Genesis 1:28). Jesus, speaking about being fruitful, declared, "By their fruits ye shall know them" (Matthew 7:16, ASV).

Investor Warren Buffett reminds us, "Should you find yourself in a chronically leaking boat, energy devoted to changing vessels is likely to be more productive than energy devoted to patching leaks."[3] In other words, be wise in your productive efforts by focusing on the right priorities.

As you go through your season of trouble, are you staying productive? As you deal with the challenges of emotional captivity, do you continue to produce a harvest that will glorify God?

Pray for Your Enemy's Prosperity

The captive Israelites were also told to pray for the prosperity of their captors (Jeremiah 29:7). That seems like a strange thing to do. Why would you want those who have confined and disrupted your life to do well? Faith in God's providence enables us to have a magnanimous spirit.

The young Israelite girl who served as a maid to General Naaman's wife had such a spirit (2 Kings 5). Though a prisoner of war, she felt sympathy for her captor, who was afflicted with dreadful leprosy. She knew of the prophet Elisha's power, that he could heal her master, and she didn't keep this secret to herself. She told her mistress how Naaman could be healed—thus working and praying for the prosperity of her captor.

How do you handle your enemies? How often do you pray for them? Jesus challenges us: "Love your enemies, bless those who curse you, do good to those who hate you, and pray for those who spitefully use you" (Matthew 5:44, NKJV). If you learn to pray for those who take advantage of you, you will honor God, and He will honor your obedience.

AN ACTION PLAN TO HELP YOU TRUST GOD'S PLAN

> *Surrender to God's providence.*

> *Believe in God's kindness.*

> *Accept God's chastisement.*

> *Live with hope.*

> *Believe God's revelation over human speculation.*

> *Seek God with intensity.*

> *Stay productive.*

> *Pray for your enemy's prosperity.*

3

MEET THE CHALLENGES
OF DARK DAYS

HAVE YOU EVER WONDERED if your dark days of trouble will end? Have you ever felt like whatever hope you once had has dried up like a raisin in the sun? Have you ever felt like giving up because one trial seems to follow another in quick succession? If you responded yes to any of these questions, let me encourage you to believe that you can find blessings in your life's dark seasons.

The pathway to blessing begins when you learn to surrender control of your life to God, when you learn the nature of true prayer. As you grow to love Him more, you should expect your loving heavenly Father to dispel your darkness. You'll then be able to relax and enjoy His plan for your life.

Develop the Right Perspective
To prepare for dark days, you must develop the right perspective on life's recurring trials. Trouble and darkness are part of the

human condition, so don't panic or become discouraged by repetitive seasons of hardship. Dark days are a natural part of life.

The greatest heroes of the faith encountered trouble, even after walking with God for decades. The upright and faithful Job finally concluded, "How frail is humanity! How short is life, how full of trouble!" (Job 14:1, NLT). Moses buckled under the murmuring of the Israelites in the latter years of his life and in the anger of disobedience struck a rock that God had commanded him only to speak to (Numbers 20). Daniel was sent to the lion's den when he was at least eighty years old (Daniel 6).

With a right perspective on trouble, you'll remember that God has placed limits on the evil that can come your way. This should give you confidence as you encounter life's difficulties because you know God has already weighed the challenge and knows that you have the strength to meet it. When the devil wanted to afflict Job, it was God who established the boundaries to this testing (Job 1). He will not permit you to be tested beyond your powers to endure (1 Corinthians 10:13).

The right perspective on trouble also enables you to see life's tribulations as opportunities for God to demonstrate His power and show Himself strong. Think about it: If God kept you from going through major difficulties, you would not know the extent and majesty of His power. Jesus told His disciples that the death of Lazarus was an opportunity for them to believe (John 11) and that the man who was born blind (John 9) had spent his life in darkness so that the works of God might be manifested in him.

We can also take comfort in the fellowship of suffering by remembering that whatever we're going through, others are bearing similar burdens. Avoid Elijah's "lone ranger" attitude (1 Kings 19). He became discouraged and deluded himself into believing he was the only person going through a particular trial. He said to God,

"I'm the only one left who hasn't bowed down to the idol Baal."
Don't make the mistake of thinking you've been singled out for
suffering, testing, or persecution. Whatever your predicament, it
is common to humanity (1 Corinthians 10:13).

Some challenges we face are external—traps, enemies, seduc-
tions, and persecutions—but others percolate within our own
hearts. James says we're tempted when we're drawn to something
by our own internal lust (James 1:14). In other words, quit blam-
ing the devil for everything. As creatures "born in sin and shaped
in iniquity" (Psalm 51:5), some of our troubles are rooted within
us. In *Phaedrus*, Plato describes the human soul as a chariot drawn
by two winged horses—one noble, the other ignoble—each pull-
ing in the opposite direction. In other words, a civil war brews
inside of each one of us.

Developing the right perspective on trouble can lead us to
appreciate our trials. Trials humble us, puncturing our pride and
bringing us to greater dependence on God. They remind us of
past mistakes, leading us to firmly resolve to do better. They make
us able to empathize. We develop the ability to walk for a while
in someone else's shoes, discarding our judgmental arrogance on
the trash heap, where it belongs. Peter is far more humble and
dependent on Jesus in John 21, after he has denied Him three
times, than he was in Luke 22, before his denials. He benefited
from his trials.

Relinquish Control

After gaining the proper perspective on your troubles, meet the
challenges of dark days by relinquishing control of your life. Jesus
hinted at this principle when He declared that those who seek to
save their lives will lose them, but those who are willing to lose
their lives for His sake will find them (Matthew 16:25). God wants

us to trust Him to order our steps and direct our paths. Perhaps that's why we're admonished to lean not on our own understanding (Proverbs 3:5-6), but to trust God to choreograph our steps. Romans 8 picks up this theme, informing us that we don't know how to pray or what to pray for, so why not relinquish control to the Holy Spirit, who does know how to intercede on our behalf?

Refusing to relinquish control to God is foolish because He knows what the future holds and we don't. We don't even know what a day will bring forth (Proverbs 27:1), but God does. Even if we knew what would happen tomorrow, we often don't know what is best for us and our loved ones.

Fortunately for us, God sometimes says no. I once asked God to permit me to grow up and make one hundred dollars a week. "If You'll just do this," I pleaded, "I'll never ask You for anything else for as long as I live." I'm glad He said no. Had He answered my prayer and capped my salary at that paltry sum, I would now be most pitiable.

Discover the Nature of True Prayer

How passionate are you about prayer? Do you see it as a privilege? Imagine its awesomeness. We are permitted to enter God's throne room, to have a private audience with the Creator, to tap into omnipotent power that can deliver us from principalities and powers. Do you value this great blessing?

If you do, I encourage you to become a student of prayer. C. H. Dodd once said that true prayer enables God within us to connect with God above us. Romans 8:26 seems to suggest this same sentiment when it says, "The Holy Spirit prays for us with groanings that cannot be expressed in words" (NLT). Indeed, we have God within us to connect us to God above us.

Do you trust the Holy Spirit to pray for you? When you do,

you're actually surrendering to God's wisdom, saying, "Lord, I don't trust my judgment more than Yours, so have Your way." You're joining with the hymnist who wrote, "Thou art the Potter; I am the clay." When you trust God to pray for you, you honor Him by suggesting that your trust in Him is so complete that you'll leave the results to His loving providence. That is the nature of true prayer. It is not to change God, but to transform you and me, making us surrender our wills to the One who hung the stars in space.

Allow God to Transform Your Dark Yesterdays

God has promised to transform our dark yesterdays. Romans 8:28 says it this way: "In all things God works for the good of those who love him, who have been called according to his purpose" (NIV). What an amazing promise! Nothing can happen to us from which God cannot eventually bring good. He can bring blessings from sickness, unemployment, guilt, shame, betrayal, and sorrow. Whatever shadows darken your yesterdays can be lifted. Perhaps Psalm 27:1 refers to this: "The Lord is my light and my salvation. Whom then shall I fear?" God is our light. He illumines the paths over which He takes us. He then brings us to a plateau, where, looking back, we see our pain from His perspective. We then see the goodness of our afflictions, the blessings in our setbacks. We're then able to say with Joseph, "You meant it for evil, but God meant it for good" (Genesis 50:20).

James Russell Lowell knew that God could bring good out of evil. He writes, "Truth forever on the scaffold, wrong forever on the throne—yet that scaffold sways the future, and, behind the dim unknown, standeth God within the shadow, keeping watch above his own."[4] Lowell seems to be suggesting that God's purposes can't be stopped. Like the coming of the morning, which cannot be restrained, God's purposes will ultimately prevail.

Make Loving God Your Top Priority

To ensure that God's purposes will ultimately prevail in your life, make loving Him your top priority. Romans 8:28 says that God's purposes are realized in the lives of those who love Him. This means that those who have developed a relationship with God will stay in His will, so that His purposes will prevail. We can almost feel Joseph's passion and love for God in his rebuff of Potiphar's wife's overtures: "How then can I do this great wickedness and sin against God?" (Genesis 39:9, esv). Joseph's resistance sends him to jail and forces him to wait years for justice. But when God decides to move, Joseph goes from prison to prime minister in less than twenty-four hours. God can bring you from prison to preeminence.

Have you made loving God your top priority? It means developing a relationship with Him, through prayer and studying His Word, and enjoying His presence. When you do this, you'll discover that He can transform the worst trouble into an oasis of peace and enable you to meet the challenges of your darkest days.

AN ACTION PLAN TO HELP YOU MEET THE CHALLENGES OF DARK DAYS

> *Develop the right perspective.*

> *Relinquish control.*

> *Discover the nature of true prayer.*

> *Allow God to transform your dark yesterdays.*

> *Make loving God your top priority.*

4

RESTORE BROKEN WALLS

THE STORY OF NEHEMIAH rebuilding Jerusalem's walls provides one of the greatest examples of turning adversity into advantage. This great leader accomplished in fifty-two days a task that others had been attempting to accomplish for nearly a century. Isn't that amazing? Let me tell you the story.

Jerusalem and its Temple were burned and destroyed in 586 BC (2 Kings 25). This presented serious problems because the enemy destroyed Jerusalem's walls. Without walls, the people were vulnerable to attack and couldn't feel safe from their enemies.

Over decades, three major efforts were launched to rebuild Jerusalem's walls, but each failed. The fourth attempt, made by Nehemiah in 445 BC, met with success. He completed the work in less than two months.

Opposition accompanied Nehemiah's success. He received threats and attacks from various enemies who launched determined and aggressive interference. The fact that Nehemiah restored the walls in spite of these formidable foes reveals a strategy for restoring other "broken walls" in our lives.

If you've gone through tough times, most likely you've encountered broken walls—where something that once brought security is now broken, burned, and destroyed. Sometimes relationship walls break down and the regard we should have for our neighbors, or even for our loved ones, disappears. At other times, difficult circumstances threaten to devastate our faith walls. We find ourselves losing confidence in God's loving providence, and words of pessimism and cynicism begin to dominate our conversations. Others know the tragedy of a breach in their purity walls. After a life of sterling integrity, they make an ethical misstep and do something morally stupid, risking and sometimes ruining a reputation that took years to build. We need to restore these broken walls.

What about holiness walls? Remember how intense your fervor for God used to be? But now, like the members of the Ephesian church (Revelation 2), you've lost your first love and need to rebuild your holiness walls. For others, prayer walls have been compromised. You've become too busy to spend quality time conversing with God, and your prayer walls need rebuilding. What does Nehemiah teach us about restoring broken walls?

Be Passionate about Change
The plight of the Jewish remnant that survived Jerusalem's destruction caused Nehemiah to passionately desire a change (Nehemiah 1:1-4). The Bible says he sat, wept, fasted, and prayed. That's real passion. This good man mourned and began to dream about solving a seemingly unsolvable problem. When was the last time you cried about an overwhelming challenge?

It's amazing the difference that passion can make when it comes to finding blessing in adversity and celebrating our troubles. When

I was a teenager, President John F. Kennedy announced his great desire to have America send a person safely to the moon and back. The target date to make his dream a reality was set for the end of the 1960s. It seemed an impossible undertaking to me and others, but many people caught the president's contagious passion. Soon they began working diligently to do what many said couldn't be done. And guess what? They did it. Passion made a significant difference.

I'm fond of watching the Biography channel on cable television. The peaks and valleys of great lives fascinate me, particularly the ups and downs in the life of Albert Einstein. In a documentary on his life, I saw how passionately this great scientist pursued the discovery of his theory of relativity. Repeatedly, Einstein seemed to take two steps forward and three steps back. His journey toward discovery had many twists and turns, and I became exhausted just watching him work through one challenge after another. Finally he reached his goal, turning adversity into advantage because he was propelled by an unstoppable desire for change.

Beware of reaching for your dreams when this passion is absent. A journalist once asked Secretary of State Colin Powell, "Why haven't you decided to run for the U.S. presidency?"

"I don't have the fire in my belly," Powell immediately responded. This wise national leader seemed to know that anyone attempting to climb the mountain of presidential ambition must be certain that he or she desperately wants to get to the summit.

My mother possessed the necessary "fire in the belly" for her ambitions. She wanted her eight children to receive a Christian education, but Christian school tuition is expensive and she had insufficient funds. But a fire burned in the heart of Pearline Black with a heat that enabled her to do the seemingly impossible. At one point, four of her children were in Christian boarding schools simultaneously, with an educational cost that competed with her annual income of welfare checks. How she managed to realize her dream of a Christian education for all her children still baffles me. But I'm certain that her intense passion for change enabled her to move her mountains and overcome her circumstances.

What do you dream of accomplishing? Will you permit a passion for change to enable you to experience God's blessings in your adversity and, like Nehemiah, do more than you can imagine? For starters, don't underestimate the power of passion, for God said to Israel, "You will seek and find me when you seek me with all your heart" (Jeremiah 29:13, NIV).

Ask God for Favor

When you earnestly seek God, be sure to ask Him for favor. That's what Nehemiah did. He asked God for the ability to win approval. He wanted the king to desire to extend kindness to him. Nehemiah prayed, "O Lord, I pray, please let Your ear be attentive to the prayer of Your servant . . . and let Your servant prosper this day, I pray, and grant him mercy in the sight of this man" (Nehemiah 1:11, NKJV). God answered Nehemiah's prayer.

Do you need the ability to win approval? Daniel did. While he was in Babylon, he resolved not to defile himself with the king's food or wine (Daniel 1:8). How did God respond to this fidelity? Daniel 1:9 records that God brought Daniel into tender love and favor with the king's key administrator, reminding us that "the righteous are surrounded with the shield of God's favor" (Psalm 5:12).

Don't be afraid to ask God for favor. James 4:2 says, "You have not because you ask not." Why would you miss a blessing simply because you failed to request it? Nehemiah turned adversity into advantage by asking God for favor.

Once, while walking through an airport, I spotted a young man wearing a T-shirt with this message printed on the back: "Don't envy me. Favor isn't fair." How true! God permitted Solomon, the son of David and Bathsheba, to become Israel's king instead of one of his brothers. Solomon acknowledged God's kindness and favor in one of his prayers (1 Kings 3), for he had received the divine gift of undeserved preeminence. Favor isn't fair.

Once I received orders to work for a man who didn't like me. My friends expressed their condolences when they learned of my plight. "The Lord have mercy on you, Barry," they moaned, as they shook their heads pessimistically. I didn't know what to do, because military orders required me to accept this new assignment. So I prayed and asked God for favor.

Arriving at my new assignment, my introduction to my new boss began poorly. He seemed rude and unfriendly. The weeks flew by, and he rarely spoke a civil word to me. One morning as I entered my office, the executive assistant called out to me with alarm in her voice, "The boss wants to see you immediately."

I entered his office with trepidation and stood at attention beside his desk. He looked up at me and then looked down, only to continue writing. Finally, he spoke: "I don't know why I like you!" He almost spat out the words.

"I don't understand, sir," I responded.

"You should," he barked. "I don't know why I like you. You may leave; that will be all."

Executing a brisk about-face and leaving his office, I thought, *I know why you like me. I've been blessed with God's favor. He's answered my prayer.* The favor of God brought blessing from adversity.

Be Prepared for Doors of Opportunity to Open

Would you be ready if your door of opportunity opened right now? Many of us wouldn't, but Nehemiah was ready. After four months of passionate concern, one day the king said to him, "What is it you want?" (Nehemiah 2:4, NIV).

Nehemiah quickly prayed and then answered, "Send me to the city in Judah where my fathers are buried so that I can rebuild it" (Nehemiah 2:5, NIV).

Wow! Just like that, Nehemiah asked for permission to solve a century-old problem.

His preparation ran deeper than this request. He also asked for a letter from the king so that he wouldn't be stopped along the way. He then requested a second letter. This one would go to the keeper of the king's forest so that Nehemiah would have the timber needed for restoring the broken walls.

Preparation continued when Nehemiah arrived in Jerusalem. He set out during the night with a few men to personally inspect the devastated walls and the burned gates (Nehemiah 2:11-13).

I'll ask you again, would you be ready if your door of opportunity opened right now?

I really wasn't ready for my big break. I'd been asked to interview for the U.S. Senate chaplain's position, but I hadn't done my homework. Two days before my first interview, I learned how unprepared I was.

I was in a military transition assistance class that prepared admirals and generals to reenter civilian life. When one of my instructors heard I'd be interviewing for the chaplain's job in forty-eight hours, he said, "Why don't we role-play Barry's interview?" The class chuckled, and I reluctantly left my seat and sat at the front of the class.

Thank God this is not the actual interview, I thought.

My inquisitor fired his first question: "Barry, who's on the Senate selection committee that will interview you?"

I reflected before replying and said, "I won't know that until I'm interviewed in two days."

My questioner smiled. "Why is it that I already know the names of the senators on your selection committee, and yet I'm not the one being interviewed for the job?"

"I haven't the foggiest idea," I said with some puzzlement.

"Well, I found the information on a Senate Web site, and you could've done the same."

I felt some embarrassment as my classmates smiled, amused by my subpar performance. But I also breathed a sigh of relief; at least there was still time to prepare.

The role-playing continued and my relentless interviewer pummeled me with more questions that I answered poorly. When he'd finished, I rushed home to prepare, spending the next two days as if cramming for a final exam. I thanked God that I had learned an important lesson before it cost me my opportunity: To fail to prepare is to prepare to fail. Forty-eight hours later, when real senators fired their questions, I was drowsy but prepared.

Even the great apostle Paul had to prepare for his opportunities. After his Damascus Road conversion (Acts 9), he spent three years in the Arabian desert preparing for his apostolic work (Galatians 1:16-18). Prepare, prepare, prepare. Those who would find blessing in adversity must be prepared when opportunity knocks.

In a speech to African American youth, Martin Luther King Jr. challenged them to be ready when the doors of opportunity opened. This preparation entailed striving for excellence with the tasks at hand, doing one's work so well "that the living, the dead, or the unborn couldn't do it any better."[5] That's preparing for opportunities in the manner of Nehemiah.

Expect Opposition

Change doesn't roll in on the wheels of inevitability, and rarely are laudable goals reached without opposition. In Nehemiah's experience, "When Sanballat heard that we were rebuilding the wall, he became angry and was greatly incensed. He ridiculed the Jews" (Nehemiah 4:1, NIV). There it is—opposition.

At the time of this writing, the U.S. Congress has just passed sweeping health-care reform. It's an initiative that people have attempted to complete since the Truman Administration. Regardless of your political leanings, you probably remember that the legislative process that gave birth to this bill was full of great opposition.

David encountered opposition when he spoke out against Goliath (1 Samuel 17). While all of Israel trembled with fear, David asked, "Who is this uncircumcised Philistine that he should defy the armies of the living God?" (verse 26, NIV). David's older brother immediately opposed him, saying, "Why did you come down here? And with whom have you left those few sheep in the wilderness? I know your pride and the insolence of your heart, for you have come down to see the battle" (verse 28, NKJV).

Sure enough, opposition besets most laudable initiatives. In fact, God guarantees opposition for those who live right. Second Timothy 3:12 states, "All those who live a godly life will suffer persecution." So be like Nehemiah and find advantage in your adversity. Say hooray for trouble as you defeat your opposition.

AN ACTION PLAN TO HELP YOU
RESTORE BROKEN WALLS

> *Be passionate about change.*

> *Ask God for favor.*

> *Be prepared for doors of opportunity to open.*

> *Expect opposition.*

5

BENEFIT FROM BROKENNESS

Behold, blessed is the one whom God reproves;
therefore despise not the discipline of the Almighty.

JOB 5:17, ESV

I HAVE SEEN AND FELT LIFE'S ADVERSITIES. I once witnessed a difficult season as I stood in a gloomy hospital corridor while a wife and mother—who had already buried her eldest daughter due to an automobile accident—waited and hoped and prayed that her husband might not die.

But he did.

And while his funeral was in progress later the next week, I witnessed grief that opened the floodgates of my tears.

I felt brokenness standing at the bedside of my father when he died, watching as doctors rushed into the room in response to an emergency code that summoned them to attempt to resuscitate him. I wondered about expending such diligence on someone who had already been classified as terminal.

I saw brokenness when a twenty-three-year-old man was murdered three days after he had accepted Christ. As I delivered the eulogy at his funeral, I questioned whether, indeed, "all things work together for the good of those who love the Lord" (Romans 8:28).

I feel brokenness like a nagging toothache when I read about the tragedies of war and recall my twenty-seven years of military service, which prompted me to wrestle with the wisdom of warfare in a nuclear age. When I see gang violence in America's inner cities, or the tragic poverty in the subcultures of many urban centers, or the epidemic of high school dropouts among many ethnic minorities, or the domestic turmoil that fuels a skyrocketing divorce rate, I feel brokenness.

I feel it as I react to the headlines and face the crises of our broken world. I feel it when it seems to me that too many good people are needlessly suffering. I have seen and sought to comfort too many broken hearts. Perhaps you have too.

I've seen enough anguish to convince me that evil is real; sin is pervasive, and death is a regular and frequent intruder on humanity. Yet in spite of the brokenness and suffering all around me, I believe that God can use our pain and enable us to benefit from affliction.

Though many people see primarily negatives in their troubles, benefits often come from such afflictions. They humble us, deepen our knowledge of God, strengthen our prayer lives, expose us to divine grace, enable us to see God's faithfulness, lead us to the sacred Word, deepen our appreciation of divine providence, and draw us away from backsliding. Sweet are God's uses of adversity.

Allow Affliction to Humble You

Trouble can eradicate our pride and bring humility. We saw this in the life of former Alabama governor George Wallace. This avowed segregationist, an advocate of divisive political tactics and discriminatory behavior, experienced a tragedy that placed him in a wheelchair after he barely survived a would-be assassin's bullet.

As a result, Wallace experienced constant pain and had much time to reflect. A different man emerged from this terrible ordeal. After this tragedy, Wallace exhibited such contrition and sorrow for his past behavior that he was eventually reelected as Alabama's governor with significant African American support. The people he had once vilified became allies, and Wallace transformed a negative legacy into something positive.

Long before George Wallace came on the scene, an overconfident fisherman named Peter learned that affliction can produce humility. Peter would later preach on the Day of Pentecost (Acts 2), and more than three thousand people would come to Christ as a result of his testimony. But before that could happen, he had to be humbled by the tragedy of denying his Lord three times. This denial came after he had boasted about his willingness to die for Jesus. Devastated by his flagrant sin, Peter wept bitter tears of repentance (Luke 22:62). Later, when a humbled Peter encountered Jesus after His resurrection, Jesus asked, "Peter, do you love Me more than these?" (John 21:1-17).

"Lord, You know I love You," Peter replied cautiously.

Jesus asked him the same question two more times. Each time, Peter responded with both uncertainty and humility. He almost seemed to be saying, "Lord, You know my heart. Tell me if I love You." What an amazing change from the days of his confident boasting. He was now a man whom God could use mightily because affliction had humbled him.

Allow Affliction to Deepen Your Knowledge of God

Affliction can deepen our knowledge of God, bringing us into greater intimacy with Him. Speaking about this intimacy, Job declares, "Now acquaint yourself with Him, and be at peace" (Job 22:21, NKJV). Job's declaration reminds us to get to know

God. Affliction often provides the necessary motivation for this pursuit of the transcendent. We come to know how God's providence unfolds by passing through affliction's crucible. By the time Job had gone through his labyrinthine ordeal of grief and loss, his knowledge of God had grown dramatically. He said to God, "I have heard of You by the hearing of the ear, but now my eye sees You" (Job 42:5, NKJV).

The boy Samuel had a similar experience with God. Samuel became acquainted with God through the stern voice of judgment (1 Samuel 3). He lived with Eli the priest at a time when God was about to punish Eli's family. One evening, Samuel heard a voice. Thinking it was his master, Eli, he hurried to the priest's bed. When Eli became aware that God was attempting to communicate, he instructed Samuel to say, "Speak, Lord; I'm listening." When Samuel obeyed, God spoke to him about a fierce judgment soon to fall upon Eli's sons. With trepidation, Samuel warned Eli, who accepted the news with resignation. Samuel lived to see Eli's home destroyed, but from the crucible of these afflictions blessings would come. These afflictions developed Samuel into a significant spiritual force in Israel, enabling him to become acquainted with God's sometimes mysterious ways.

Allow Affliction to Strengthen Your Prayer Life

Afflictions can strengthen your prayer life. Someone once called prayer the breath of the soul, and so it is. The prophet Elijah experienced the pain of watching Israel decide to follow the idolatrous ways of Baal, a Canaanite deity. This sorrowful trial put the prophet on his knees. He so earnestly wanted God to bring Israel to repentance that he asked God to stop the rain and send a famine. God answered his fervent prayers (James 5:17-18). It was affliction that energized the prophet's prayer life.

Jesus suggested that prayer is the antidote to despair, asserting that "people should always pray and not lose heart" (Luke 18:1).

Despair usually increases the number of prayers, thereby making it more probable that people will become better intercessors, for practice makes perfect. As we go to God repeatedly in prayer to deal with our afflictions, we become better at listening to Him and articulating our concerns. Affliction, therefore, can strengthen your prayer life.

My mother was known throughout my church community as a prayer warrior. I once asked her, "How did you develop such a powerful prayer life?"

"Praying for your daddy for thirty years," she responded. Her prayer life was strengthened by her diligent intercession for an alcoholic husband, which improved her ability to communicate with heaven.

Allow Affliction to Expose You to God's Grace

Another benefit of affliction is that it exposes us to God's grace. This is one reason why "where sin abounds, grace does much more abound" (Romans 5:20). When God comes through for us in our hour of need, it heightens our awareness of His mercies, which are new each day.

In the story of Jonah, God calls a reluctant prophet to go to Nineveh with a message of judgment. But the prophet chooses to flee in the opposite direction. Eventually, after an ordeal with a great fish, he decides to do what God asked and preaches judgment to Nineveh. But when the people heed Jonah's word and repent, it triggers Jonah's anger at God. "I knew You were merciful," he says. Jonah is angry that his prophecy regarding Nineveh's destruction had not come true.

One day, while Jonah is sitting in the sun, a plant grows quickly beside him, shading his bald head from the sun. But alas, the plant dies almost as quickly as it rose, further angering Jonah. But God is teaching Jonah a lesson about mercy. He says to Jonah, "Are you upset that the plant died? Why can't you be happy that thousands of people have been spared My judgment?" (Jonah 4:10-11). It was the painful rays of the sun that led Jonah to a better understanding of God's amazing grace.

Allow Affliction to Reveal God's Faithfulness

Affliction often helps us to see God's great faithfulness more clearly. When God told Abraham and Sarah they would have a son, they disbelieved. In fact, Sarah laughed (Genesis 18). They had not yet learned to trust God's faithfulness. When Abraham took Hagar, Sarah's Egyptian maid, as a concubine in an attempt to fulfill God's promise, Hagar bore Ishmael, bringing many problems to the household. Later, when Abraham suffered through the burden of attempting to sacrifice Isaac, he finally learned the extent of God's faithfulness. Suffering provided him with a valuable education.

David received a similar education. He writes in Psalm 37:25: "I was young and now I am old, yet I have never seen the righteous forsaken or their children begging bread" (NIV). Through life's up-and-down journey, the psalmist discovered that God takes care of His own. And over what terrain did his journey take him? For many years, David was a fugitive, experiencing unspeakable hardships. His enemies kidnapped his family, burned his home, and destroyed everything he owned (1 Samuel 30). Yet through all these setbacks, he found blessings in adversity by discovering God's dependability and faithfulness.

We all can discover God's faithfulness through suffering. We can be certain about His faithfulness: "God is not a man, that He should lie, nor a son of man, that He should repent. Has He said, and will He not do? Or has He spoken, and will He not make it good?" (Numbers 23:19, NKJV).

Allow Affliction to Lead You to God's Word

King David discovered that affliction can often lead us to God's Word. In Psalm 119, he writes, "Before I was afflicted I went astray, but now I obey your word" (verse 67, NIV); "It was good for me to be afflicted so that I might learn your decrees" (verse 71, NIV); and, "Your word is a lamp to my feet and a light for my path" (verse 105, NIV).

During my turbulent teen years, I rebelled against the restraints of my Christian home. I said to my mother, "I'm tired of going to Christian schools. I'm a man and can do what I please." Eventually, she relented and allowed me to attend public school. It wasn't long before I joined a gang. This foolish decision took me into dangerous and immoral places until I sustained injuries during a gang fight. My physical suffering compelled me to flee back to my biblical roots, as I beat a hasty path back to church school. I applied myself to my studies as never before, graduating valedictorian of my class, devouring Scripture, and memorizing long passages. Afflictions brought me back to God's Word.

Allow Affliction to Deepen Your Trust in God's Providence

If you trust God passionately, always seeking His will, He will direct your steps (Proverbs 3:5-6). God's guidance often comes through afflictions that deepen our appreciation for His providential leading.

Joseph's story shows this beautifully, for his life was divinely directed (Genesis 37–50). Whether in the pit awaiting his fate, sold as a slave by his brothers, betrayed by Potiphar's wife, or unfairly incarcerated, he continued to trust God's loving providence. In the end, he acknowledged that God had transformed his afflictions into blessings (Genesis 50).

Many years later, a shepherd named David learned to trust God's guidance in his life. After receiving a special consecration as Israel's future king (1 Samuel 16), he found himself on the run as a fugitive for many years. This wilderness time in his life helped David develop a dependence on God during the more than thirty years that elapsed between his anointing and coronation as Israel's king. God led him on a circuitous route, but one that prepared him for his great responsibility. Afflictions bless us when we find directions for life's journey along the way.

Allow Affliction to Bring You Back to God

Often affliction brings us back from the far country of the backslider. This is clearly seen in the parable of the Prodigal Son (Luke 15). This wayward boy received his inheritance and then squandered it in a far country. For a while, things went swimmingly. Surrounded by friends and well-wishers, he lived a five-star life—until the money ran out. Then he began to know the pain of poverty. In desperation, he accepted a job tending pigs—a great humiliation for any self-respecting Jew. He hit rock bottom, with no place to go but up. And when he remembered his father's house, he decided to return home.

How true this sequence is for many backsliders. Like Samson, who squandered God's blessing through a sinful relationship, most prodigals stray from godly principles for living and eventually face painful consequences (Judges 16). After Samson fell, he served as a slave, deprived of his sight by Philistine brutality. Through the valley of these afflictions, Samson found his way back to spiritual fitness, ultimately fulfilling God's purpose for his life. Affliction brought him the blessings of repentance and restoration.

Joni Eareckson Tada has experienced her share of afflictions. As a teenager, she became a quadriplegic after a tragic accident. Totally dependent on others, unable to eat or drink or even wipe away her tears without assistance, she experienced anger and depression. By the grace of God, however, she eventually became a passionate advocate for the disabled, speaking, writing, and singing, and inspiring people to help the less fortunate. Joni once said, "Afflictions will either warm you up toward spiritual things or turn you cold." Thankfully, she allowed her afflictions to ignite a fire that drew her closer to God and has blessed many. We should do no less with our own afflictions.

AN ACTION PLAN TO HELP YOU BENEFIT FROM BROKENNESS

> *Allow affliction to humble you.*

> *Allow affliction to deepen your knowledge of God.*

> *Allow affliction to strengthen your prayer life.*

> *Allow affliction to expose you to God's grace.*

> *Allow affliction to reveal God's faithfulness.*

> *Allow affliction to lead you to God's Word.*

> *Allow affliction to deepen your trust in God's providence.*

> *Allow affliction to bring you back to God.*

6

REFUSE TO WASTE SUFFERING

When I was young, I memorized the following poem:

I walked a mile with pleasure,
She chatted all the way;
But left me none the wiser
For all she had to say.
I walked a mile with sorrow,
And ne'er a word said she.
But oh! The things I learned from her,
When sorrow walked with me.

What have you learned from your suffering? Suffering that doesn't teach a lesson can be considered wasted. If you go through a painful experience and learn nothing, you're very likely to repeat that painful encounter.

What does it mean to be brokenhearted? It means to be overcome by grief or despair, like Adam and Eve were after their son Cain killed his brother, Abel (Genesis 4). It's what Jacob experienced when he mistakenly thought that his son Joseph had been killed by a wild beast (Genesis 37). Jesus was overwhelmed with grief after the death of His friend Lazarus (John 11:35). Life's seasons inevitably bring brokenheartedness.

Have you experienced the brokenness of suffering? Have you seen bends in life's road that were placed there by God to bless you? Have you known experiences that have irritated and hurt you, but made you better? It may have been an illness or the loss of someone close to you. Perhaps your present brokenness involves personal failure, an academic setback, or vocational disappointment. Maybe your brokenness has to do with a rumor circulating in your office or church or neighborhood, damaging your reputation and undoing years of faithful labor. It may be that your suffering comes from anxiety about physical symptoms that your physician doesn't even know about. Whatever the source, don't waste your sufferings.

Why should we not waste our sufferings? Primarily because they have the power to purge us of impurities. Joseph's brothers experienced such a purging in Genesis 37–50. In their early days, they felt homicidal jealousy toward Joseph and eventually sold him into slavery. They lied to their father about their cowardly act and suggested that a wild beast must have killed their brother. As the years came and went, Joseph's brothers suffered from the guilt of their evil deed, until they finally reached a point at which they were purged of their jealousy and covetousness. Because of the pain of guilt and privation, they developed such ethical maturity that they were willing to sacrifice for one another. Suffering purged them of their moral impurities.

The late Archbishop Fulton Sheen, commenting on the word

sincere, said the following: "When the Romans found pieces of marble that were imperfect, they put wax in the holes. Wax, in Latin, is *cera*. When they found a perfect piece of marble, it was called *sine cera*, or without wax, whence comes the word 'sincere.'"[6] In a similar way, sufferings purge the impure wax from our lives, enabling us to become more spiritually fit and ethically mature.

James 1:2-4 expresses this idea: "Consider it pure joy, my brothers, whenever you face trials of many kinds, because you know that the testing of your faith develops perseverance. Perseverance must finish its work so that you may be mature and complete, not lacking anything" (NIV). In this passage, the Greek word for testing is *dokimion*, a word used to describe sterling coinage, when money is genuine. Sufferings can burn away the dross in our lives and make us genuine spiritual currency for God's glory.

Second, we should not waste sufferings because they can provide us with strength for greater challenges. Your willingness to endure present afflictions equips you for success when facing future difficulties. When David appeared before King Saul and volunteered to fight Goliath, he received little encouragement (1 Samuel 17). He had been Saul's armor bearer and musician (1 Samuel 16), hardly a top candidate for one-on-one combat. King Saul said to him, "You can't fight this giant and succeed. You're just a boy, and he's a combat veteran" (1 Samuel 17:33).

David refused to be intimidated. Instead, he reminded Saul of past challenges and hardships he had successfully managed. "Your servant keeps his father's sheep," David said. "And while I labored, God delivered me from a lion's clutches and a bear's paws. This Philistine giant will be like one of those beasts" (1 Samuel 17:34-36). King Saul was unaware of the sufferings and challenges David had already faced and conquered that would equip him to succeed against the giant.

One old hymn puts it this way: "Yield not to temptation, for yielding is sin. Each victory will help you some other to win."[7] That's so true. As we persevere through our current testing, we're being strengthened for future challenges. Jeremiah says it another way: "If you have raced with men on foot and they have worn you out, how can you compete with horses? If you stumble in safe country, how will you manage in the thickets by the Jordan?" (Jeremiah 12:5, NIV). In other words, we must win small victories to prepare for greater challenges.

Third, we should not waste sufferings because they can bring us the blessing of God's presence. We see this in the case of Stephen, one of Christianity's first deacons and first martyrs (Acts 6–7). Stephen faithfully served God, meeting frequent and fierce opposition. When he was arrested and brought before the high council, he felt the sustaining presence of God's glory. The Bible records that his face shone like an angel (Acts 6:15), and that he saw the heavens opened and Jesus standing at God's right hand (Acts 7:56). Even when Stephen's enemies decided to kill him, picking up stones to strike him down, his suffering brought him into the wonderful presence of God.

So there you have it: three reasons not to waste your sufferings. Sufferings purge impurities, strengthen us for greater challenges, and bring us God's glorious presence. We see these same three factors in the lives of the many Bible heroes and heroines who didn't waste their sufferings: Abraham, Isaac, Jacob, Joseph, Moses, Esther, Ruth, Elijah, and Job. The list could go on and on.

Expect Suffering

If these blessings are available when you don't waste your sufferings, what should you do? Expect sufferings. Jesus promised His disciples that they would suffer. He said, "In the world you will have tribulation" (John 16:33, NKJV). Paul expressed a similar sentiment in 2 Timothy 3:12: "All those who live godly lives will suffer persecution." Stop trying to escape the inevitability of sufferings and learn to benefit from them.

See Suffering as a Test

If we have the right perspective on suffering, we will see it as testing. "For those whom the Lord loves He disciplines, and He scourges every son whom He receives" (Hebrews 12:6, NASB). Perhaps this is what Jesus was alluding to when He told Peter, "The devil desires to sift you like wheat" (Luke 22:31). Jesus wanted Peter to see his impending trouble as a test that would ultimately bless him.

How should we respond to such testing? It helps to ask some questions. First, how am I responding to this test? Second, how should I respond to it? And finally, am I learning from this painful experience? These questions provide an appropriate response to the test of suffering.

Discover a Deeper Fellowship with Jesus Christ

Suffering can lead you to a greater intimacy with Christ, enabling you to identify with some of the trials he endured. Have you ever been betrayed? So was Jesus. Have you ever been stripped of your dignity? So was Jesus. Have you ever been forsaken by your friends, or falsely accused, or had your words misinterpreted, or been the victim of malicious gossip? So was Jesus.

Our sufferings are what enable us to identify with the Savior's life. Though we may never have nails driven through our hands or a spear thrust in our sides, we can show our love for Jesus by greeting our pain with the same equanimity He showed in meeting His agony. The apostle Paul describes this quest in the following way: "I want to know Christ and the power of his resurrection and the fellowship of sharing in his sufferings, becoming like him in his death, and so, somehow, to attain to the resurrection from the dead" (Philippians 3:10-11, NIV). Redeem your suffering by allowing it to deepen your intimacy with Jesus.

A great life can inspire us and empower us to endure hardships. Knute Rockne was the coach of the University of Notre Dame football team in the 1920s, and George Gipp was his star player. As the story goes, Gipp fell ill, and when he knew he was dying, he asked Rockne to promise that, when things were going badly for the team, he would inspire them by asking them to "win one for the Gipper." Sure enough, in a game that Notre Dame was losing, their coach reminded them of George Gipp's request. The memory and love of their teammate were sufficient to inspire the beleaguered team to rise to victory. As Christians, we have the significant inspiration of Jesus' life to spur us on. If we'll permit our sufferings to deepen our fellowship with our risen Lord, time and again we'll win one for the Master.

In *As You Like It*, Shakespeare observes, "Sweet are the uses of adversity; which, like the toad, ugly and venomous, wears yet a precious jewel in his head; and this our life, exempt from public haunt, finds tongues in trees, books in the running brooks, sermons in stones, and good in everything."[8] Those who waste their sufferings rarely smell the perfume of adversity that enables them to uncover the good in everything. They miss opportunities to experience the joy of Paul's declaration, "In everything God is working for the good of those who love Him and are called according to His purposes" (Romans 8:28).

AN ACTION PLAN TO HELP YOU REFUSE TO WASTE SUFFERING

> *Expect suffering.*

> *See suffering as a test.*

> *Discover a deeper fellowship with Jesus Christ.*

7

ACCEPT THE INEVITABILITY
OF TROUBLE

THE LYRICS OF AN OLD JOE SOUTH SONG, popularized in a 1970 rendition by Lynn Anderson, declare matter-of-factly, "I beg your pardon; I never promised you a rose garden." These words speak to the inevitability of troubles in life.

Have you been expecting life to be a rose garden? In his poem "A Psalm of Life," Henry Wadsworth Longfellow declares, "Life is real! Life is earnest!" Life is more like a wild, overgrown forest in which we can certainly expect to encounter troubles, trials, and tests than it is like a carefully maintained garden, protected from pests and predators. Remember Job's perspective: "How frail is humanity! How short is life, how full of trouble!" (Job 14:1, NLT). To be sure, if you're living right, the Bible promises you'll have trouble. Listen to the words of the apostle Paul, no stranger to trouble himself: "Anyone who belongs to Christ Jesus and wants to live right will have trouble from others" (2 Timothy 3:12).

Paul indicates that if we have a trouble-free existence, then either we don't belong to Christ or we have no desire to live right. But any true Christian who strives to live in God's will can expect to experience trouble from others.

Trouble does not always come from the hand of another individual, and it can come during seasons of abundance as well as during seasons of lack. Luke 12 describes a certain rich man who had an especially bountiful harvest one year. His fields produced so much grain that he had no place to put it and needed to build additional barns. To all appearances, he had everything under control; he had enough money to solve any worldly troubles that might beset him. But he was in the dark about one important fact: He would die that night, leaving all his money behind.

Sometimes abundance itself brings trouble. It can cause people to be envious, as King Saul was of David's successes (1 Samuel 18:8-9), or tempt them to live an unhealthy lifestyle. It was partly to warn against the unique problems of success that the British poet Rudyard Kipling wrote of "meet[ing] with Triumph and Disaster and treat[ing] those two impostors just the same." Kipling was aware that apparent success can bring as many pitfalls as apparent failure.

Avoid Resignation

Rather than expecting life to be a rose garden, learn to celebrate your troubles by embracing them. If you desire to be a person of integrity, trouble is inevitable, so greet it with composure and joy. "In everything give thanks," Paul advised the Thessalonians (1 Thessalonians 5:18, NKJV).

When Job experienced great trouble, at first he accepted it with equanimity. Though he lost his wealth, his children, and his health, he refused to curse God. After learning of the loss of his children, he sighed, "The Lord gives and takes away; blessed be the name of the Lord" (Job 1:21). But then something happened and Job changed his tone. Three friends—whom Job later called "miserable comforters"—came to visit, and they induced Job to feel that God had not been fair.

Finally, Job said, "I will fill my mouth with arguments and present my case to God" (Job 23:4). When Job moved from resignation to confrontation, God spoke. He cross-examined Job (Job 38), and with His penetrating questions He led Job to greater faith.

If you're going to celebrate your troubles, you can't accept them with resignation. Talk to God with transparent earnestness. After all, He already knows what you're thinking. Present your case to Him, with all your limited knowledge and pain. He will not let you down.

When my mother died, I felt exasperated by God and didn't try to hide it. I told Him how upset I was that my prayers seemed to have gone unanswered. I had simply desired for my mother to come out of her coma so that I could say good-bye, but that didn't happen. "You call Yourself God," I complained, "and yet You didn't answer such a simple prayer. Why should I serve You?"

In His own time, God made His purposes clear to me. He helped me to see that my mother's death brought unanticipated blessings and that He hadn't made a mistake. He even enabled me to receive a one-hour video of my mother that I hadn't seen before, which brought me great comfort. Just as He revealed Himself to Job, so He made His will clear to me.

Though troubles are inevitable, it isn't necessary to resign ourselves to them. The Bible tells us to pray about everything and to make our requests known to God (Philippians 4:6-7). You can go boldly before God's throne in prayer and receive comfort and guidance (Hebrews 4:16).

Tame Your Temper

Perhaps you don't feel tempted to respond to your troubles with resignation, but with anger. That's what Esau did. After Jacob tricked him and took away his birthright, Esau angrily planned to kill his brother, declaring, "After my father dies, I'll kill Jacob" (Genesis 27:41). Later, he learned the error of his thinking and he reconciled with Jacob. Don't respond to trouble with anger.

After the 9/11 terrorist attacks in the United States, there was a great outpouring of anger from many Americans. Some were so intent on revenge that they were willing to compromise certain basic constitutional rights for citizens, all in the hope of paying back the terrorists for their evil deeds. Other citizens, in the heat of their anger, even condoned prisoner torture. Anger is rarely a constructive response.

Remember Jonah's angry response to his perceived troubles? God had sent him to preach judgment to Nineveh. After initially trying to flee, Jonah had reluctantly obeyed, and the city had repented. But then Jonah became angry. He had hoped that God would destroy the city. Dejected, he went out beyond the city walls and found a hill, where he waited to see what God would do next. God permitted a vine to grow miraculously, providing the prophet shade from the summer heat. But the vine died as quickly as it had grown, prompting Jonah to respond with rage. God said to Jonah, "Do you have a right to be angry about the vine?"

"I do," he said. "I am angry enough to die" (Jonah 4:9, NIV).

God gave Jonah a valuable lesson by saying, "You were angry over the loss of a plant, but unsympathetic about the potential death of 120,000 people in this city who don't know their right hand from their left" (Jonah 4:10-11).

You make a wise decision when you refuse to respond angrily to your troubles. It doesn't mean you can't be candid with God as you pray, talking to Him about your pain and anguish. It does mean that even your complaints to God should be made with appropriate reverence.

Find Joy
James recommends a better response to your troubles than either the anger of Esau or the resignation of Job: joy. He writes, "Consider it pure joy, my brothers, whenever you face trials of many kinds" (James 1:2, NIV). Isn't this an amazing response to trouble? He is saying, in effect, "Celebrate your troubles."

You may find it easier to celebrate your troubles in hindsight. Often it's when you look back that you can see God's intentions more clearly and can say with David, "It is good for me that I have been afflicted" (Psalm 119:71, NKJV). In retrospect, Joseph's words to his brothers—"You meant it for evil, but God meant it for good" (Genesis 50:20)—will resonate more deeply with you. The challenge of celebrating troubles intentionally is greatest when the storms of trouble first arrive and you're clueless as to what God may have in mind. And yet that is when a joyful attitude most honors Him.

When Paul and Silas landed in the Philippian jail, they knew little about what God was doing. They had been beaten until the blood coagulated in their wounds. Then they were placed in a subterranean cell, with their hands and feet immobilized by stocks. Yet in spite of their trials and tribulations, they celebrated their troubles, singing praises to God at midnight, until the prison's foundation was shaken by a miraculous earthquake. These great Christians didn't wait until God's will was clear before celebrating their troubles. They greeted their difficulties with praise.

This is exactly what they should have done because Jesus commanded it. He admonished His disciples with these words: "Happy are you when people revile and persecute you, saying all manner of evil against you falsely for My sake. Rejoice and be exceedingly glad, for great is your reward in heaven" (Matthew 5:11-12).

How does that sound? You're to be exceedingly glad. That sounds like celebrating to me. Many times while participating in Christian funerals, I've been amazed at the celebratory nature of what is often called a homegoing. People sing joyous music, and the contributions of the deceased are declared. These services remind me of the words of 1 Thessalonians 4:13: "Christians sorrow not as those who have no hope."

Do you greet your troubles with joy and celebrate with praise? Though Dr. Martin Luther King's life had been threatened, his last speech resonated with praise. He talked about having gone to the mountaintop and seen the Promised Land. "I may not get there with you," he said. "But we as a people will get to the Promised Land." He turned pain into gain by greeting his troubles with joy, and his example lives with us and inspires us to this day.

Reap the Fruit of Perseverance

When you sow seeds of joy as you face your troubles, what harvest can you expect to reap? One fruit is perseverance: "You know that when your faith is tested, your endurance has a chance to grow" (James 1:3, NLT). The ability to continue in the face of trials is a marvelous benefit. It keeps us from becoming weary in doing right, reminding us that no good is ever lost and that the harvest is certain.

Perseverance is a wonderful trait because it keeps us from quitting too soon. Often, in the weakness of our flesh, we are tempted to give up before God's plan can reach fruition. What if Joseph had quit after being sold into Egypt? What if he had simply become so discouraged that he gave up on God? This great patriarch would have missed wonderful blessings by failing to continue in the face of obstacles. He never would have become Egypt's prime minister if he had failed to persevere.

Just as greeting our troubles with joy brings perseverance, perseverance itself brings maturity and completeness (James 1:4). The English word *mature* (particularly in its use as a verb) translates the Greek word *teleios*, which is used to speak of fulfilling the purpose for which God created us. He created us for completeness or fulfillment, and when we persevere, we move down the road toward personal fulfillment.

The apostle Paul achieved this maturity and completeness in his life. Just before his death, in his final letter to his protégé Timothy, he said, "I have fought the good fight, I have finished the race, I have kept the faith. Henceforth there is laid up for me the crown of righteousness, which the Lord, the righteous judge, will award to me on that Day" (2 Timothy 4:7-8, ESV). Paul believed he had fulfilled God's purpose for his life: He had fought the good fight, finished his course, and kept the faith. He felt fulfilled as he anticipated the crown of righteousness that awaited him when God blessed him to live eternally on the other side of death.

Can you think of anyone who has fulfilled God's purpose for his or her life? Perhaps Billy Graham's name comes to mind. This great evangelist has certainly been an exemplary model of spiritual excellence. No scandal has ever been associated with his name, for he has lived a simple and productive life. Perhaps this is why he was asked to speak to the nation immediately following the tragic events of September 11, 2001.

No one fulfilled the purpose for his existence more than Jesus Christ. James Allen Francis wrote an essay titled "One Solitary Life," which refers to the impact that Jesus had. I memorized these words as a child: "All the armies that ever marched, and all the navies that

THE BLESSING OF ADVERSITY

ever were built, all the parliaments that ever sat, and all the kings that ever reigned, put together, have not affected the life of man upon this earth as powerfully as that One Solitary Life."[9] Jesus' life divided history into BC and AD, and when He shouted from the cross, "It is finished," the greatest life that was ever lived on earth came to an end, though it continues for eternity in heaven.

Our Savior fulfilled His purpose by coming to our world and dying for our sins, an act that required the spiritual fruit of perseverance and maturity. Hebrews 12:2 says that Jesus "endured the cross, despising the shame, because of the joy that was set before Him." Are you ready to reap perseverance's fruit so that you may fulfill your purpose in this life?

Harness the Power of Prayer

What do you do when there's nothing you can do? You celebrate your troubles by harnessing the power of prayer. Jesus suggested that prayer is the antidote for despair when He told the parable of the judge and the persistent widow (Luke 18:1-8) to illustrate the point that we should always pray and not lose heart. Prayer is one of our best resources when dealing with hardship.

During my teenage years, I went through a rebellious stage. I said to my mother, "I'm a man now and can come and go as I please." I began associating with the wrong crowd and joined a neighborhood gang. My mother felt powerless, for there was no male role model in our home. All she could do was pray. Sometimes when I heard her praying for me, I found myself thinking that her intercession was a waste of time. But God heard her prayers and brought me running back to sanity and right living. I'm a preacher today because my good mother prayed for me.

Is there someone for whom you should be praying? Never underestimate prayer power. The great nineteenth-century English poet Alfred, Lord Tennyson said, "More things are wrought by prayer than this world dreams of." Celebrate your troubles with prayer power. It's not an accident that Jesus' first words from the cross at Calvary took the form of a prayer for His enemies.

Ask God for Wisdom

As you celebrate your troubles with prayer power, for what should you be praying? Wisdom. James 1:5 says, "If you need wisdom, ask our generous God, and he will give it to you. He will not rebuke you for asking" (NLT). Why would anyone not seek and ask God for wisdom, when He is so eager to give it?

Wisdom is so important that when Solomon had the opportunity to receive from God the fulfillment of any request, he asked for wisdom (1 Kings 3). He later declared, "Wisdom is the principal thing; therefore get wisdom" (Proverbs 4:7, KJV). You're truly celebrating your troubles when you ask God for wisdom. For what you're actually saying through your request is this: "Guide me, O Thou great Jehovah." When we recognize that our natural intelligence is insufficient, we can ask the Giver of Wisdom to guide us through our troubles so that we might see His purpose and plan.

Remember the Past

I shouldn't have done it, but I did. As a youngster, I played the bully and took money from my childhood playmates. I intimidated them sufficiently that for weeks they didn't disclose my secret. But judgment day inevitably arrived. When they found the courage to report my playground robberies, their parents and my mother arrived on the scene to seek justice—and justice they found. My punishment was more painful than I could have ever imagined: the disappointment in my mother's tears. I would have preferred a spanking to the agony I felt as I saw my mother crying over my misdeeds.

Decades have passed, but my childhood sins and failures still haunt me. The memory of this mistake, however, has also blessed me, making me determined to never again disappoint the ones I love. Memory has the power to inspire us to live nobly and to sidestep the evil that can bring us to ruin.

Perhaps it is because memory is such a powerful force that God admonished Israel, through Moses, to remember that they were once Egyptian slaves (Deuteronomy 5:15; 15:15; 16:12; 24:18-22). Remembering a time in the past when you dealt with hardship and came through it is one of the best ways to celebrate your present trouble. Moses spoke to the Israelites just before they crossed the Jordan River into the Promised Land. As they were about to become a nation, Moses challenged them to remember their roots in slavery. When they entered the land and became rich and powerful and were living in freedom, he didn't want them to forget where they had come from. He didn't want them to forget that they had been oppressed for four hundred years, with no freedom to choose their work or where to worship. He wanted their memories to instruct them how to treat the powerless, the widows, and the foreigners who would come to their land of freedom.

Egypt represents our seasons of disadvantage, our failures, struggles, and privations. Moses' message to the Israelites applies to us, as well. Don't be afraid to revisit the shadows of your past, but also reflect on the deliverance you received and will continue to receive. The freedom God has given you enables you to consider your past in order to learn how to navigate the future. So remember Egypt.

Remembering our "Egypts" helps us appreciate God's present blessings. How often we forget the long road and the dangers, seen and unseen, over which He has given us victory. While the Israelites complained about their wilderness environment (Exodus 17:1-2), perhaps they should have remembered their Egyptian slavery experience. Before leaving Egypt, they were beaten by cruel taskmasters, forced to make bricks without straw, and subjected to a law that murdered their babies, drowning them mercilessly in the Nile River. But God rained plagues upon Egypt (Exodus 7–11), defeating Pharaoh's stubborn plans. He slew Egypt's firstborn sons and drowned its mighty army in the Red Sea. He enabled His people to make their exodus after receiving back pay for their centuries of slave labor. He gave them favor among the Egyptians, who showered them with parting gifts of gold, silver, and jewels.

In the wilderness, God guided Israel with a cloud that sheltered them from the desert sun and illumined the chilly night darkness with light and heat, enabling them to travel whenever He led them out. Remembering their slavery and God's mighty works in their history would have sweetened their present moments, but they seemed to have already forgotten these experiences. Instead, they longed for the foods they had eaten in Egypt (Numbers 11:4-6) and insulted God by distrusting His ability to care for their daily needs. We make the same mistakes today, forgetting that we were once slaves to sin and recalling our captivity as if it were a picnic to which we would like to return.

Fortunately, in earlier days, Jacob hadn't made this mistake; he remembered that his "Egypt" was no picnic. Fleeing from the anger of his twin brother, Esau, he must have felt he deserved his brother's homicidal hatred. He had taken advantage of Esau and deceived his father, Isaac, thereby gaining the family birthright, a blessing that brought wealth and power to the receiver. But one night, while filled with despair, he remembered the dangerous path over which God had sustained him and said, "With only my staff did I cross this Jordan, but God kept me and gave me great wealth" (Genesis 32:10). He connected his gratitude for present blessings to the position of disadvantage from which God had removed him. His remembering showed him his graduation from desperate fugitive to grateful child of God.

During the inaugural luncheon for President Barack Obama, I had the privilege of offering an invocation and sitting at the head table. The meal was sumptuous, with a main course of duck and pheasant (though I had arranged instead to eat a delectable vegetarian dish). Sitting and watching the wealthy and powerful in attendance, former presidents and vice presidents, members of Congress and Supreme Court justices, celebrities and foreign guests, I began to think about my Egypt. During this celebration of the orderly transition of political power, my mind took a journey to my boyhood experiences in the squalor of an inner-city public housing project. I remembered the three times my family had been evicted, our furniture placed on the sidewalk for all the neighbors to see. I recalled my embarrassment that my family's stark poverty could be seen by our neighbors, who seemed stunned that we had so little. These thoughts flashed through my mind as I greeted our new president and first lady. The memory of my past Egypt made that present moment of pomp and celebration all the more sweet.

Congressman John Lewis attended this luncheon as well. His head still bears the scars from his experience in a civil rights march as a young man, when he was brutally beaten. He handed his luncheon program to the new president, who signed it with the words, "Because of you, Barack Obama." The Egypt of the struggle for equality had passed, with the anger, police dogs, billy clubs, and fire hoses and all the hatred, fear, and despair. We could now celebrate, for God's providence had again prevailed.

Are you failing to celebrate your present troubles because you've forgotten the much worse tribulations you endured in your Egypt period? Even if you haven't experienced something as painful as grinding poverty or a physical beating, you still have an Egypt to look back on, because God has brought you from the disadvantage of a sinful past into a present salvation made possible by Jesus' death at Calvary. Each of us, therefore, has a testimony to share and memories to treasure. Remembering the depths from which Christ brought us should make us cherish the joy of daily fellowship with Him, empowering us to turn the adversity of Egypt into the advantage of a powerful witness.

Help the Helpless

Memories of Egypt should also motivate us to reach out to those on life's margins. We can easily overlook the poor and powerless, taking no significant action to relieve their plight. But remembering Egypt should keep us from making this mistake. I marvel at how often my mother and her children were invited home for Sabbath dinner after the worship service. Most of these invitations came from people who had little more than we did, but memories of their own Egypts motivated them to help this single mother and her hungry children.

Isn't it possible that this is what motivated Joseph to reach out to Pharaoh's depressed butler and baker in an Egyptian prison (Genesis 40)? Joseph had been unfairly jailed on false rape charges, triggered by the accusations of his master's wife. But instead of feeling sorry for himself, he worked with such diligence that the prison warden gave him important responsibilities, which included helping out with special prisoners. One day he noticed that two of these prisoners seemed particularly depressed, and he reached out to them. After inquiring about their condition, he was told that both were disturbed by dreams. He was able to interpret their dreams and enabled them to find peace. By the time these two prisoners were preparing to leave jail, Joseph had already spoken to one of them about his personal Egypt. He said, "I was kidnapped from my father's home and brought to this land. Now I'm jailed for something I didn't do. I really didn't deserve this treatment" (Genesis 40:15). Joseph had not forgotten his Egypt.

Does the memory of your Egypt motivate you to help those on life's margins? The woman who started the organization Mothers Against Drunk Driving (MADD) had such a motivation. After going through the trauma of her daughter's death at the hands of a drunk driver, she sought to recover from her grief by constructively using her anger. She decided to reach out to the often neglected victims of drunk drivers and their families, creating the organization MADD to make a positive difference. She permitted the memories of her Egypt to inspire her to help the helpless.

Endure Hardship
Remembering your Egypt should help you endure the trials and tribulations of life. Thinking about what God has already done makes present afflictions seem less daunting. While I was a U.S. Navy chaplain at a recruit training command, I noticed that only a few of the men and women I counseled were ethnic minorities. After a few weeks of counseling, I spoke to several African American and Latino recruits during my barracks visitation. "Why don't you guys ever come in to see me for counseling?" I asked.

"What for?" was the general response. "Chaplain, we came from cities where there were gangs and murders, and we were never sure if we'd make it home alive. This is a piece of cake compared to that." The memories of their previous hardships made the challenges of boot camp seem like light afflictions.

Before Christ's crucifixion, Peter denied Jesus (Luke 22). He later used this Egypt memory to challenge others to endure hardships with grace. He writes, "Since Christ suffered physical pain, you must arm yourselves with the same attitude he had, and be ready to suffer, too. For if you have suffered physically for Christ, you have finished with sin" (1 Peter 4:1, NLT). The memories of Jesus' sacrifice should rally our spirits. Like the Texans who cried, "Remember the Alamo," we should enter our warfare with principalities and powers (Ephesians 6:12) with a determination to pay the price of sacrifice and service, enduring hardship as good soldiers of the Cross.

Testify to God's Goodness

Remembering Egypt also provides us with a testimony. Many want a testimony without a test, but testimonies are usually forged in the furnace of affliction. God, desiring witnesses who will tell of His power and grace, often refines them with hardship. We see this in the story of the liberated demoniac (Mark 5).

This demon-possessed man had long terrorized his neighbors. He lived among the tombs, and no chains could restrain him, nor could anyone subdue him, for the demons that took his sanity also granted him superhuman strength. Day and night he ran, barely clothed, through the burial grounds, howling and cutting himself—until he encountered Jesus. He saw the Savior in the distance, ran to meet Him, and bowed. But then the demons screamed through his mouth, "Why are you interfering with me, Jesus, Son of the Most High God?" (Mark 5:7, NLT).

Jesus, ignoring this effort to sway Him from His purpose, spoke with authority to the demonic spirits that possessed this man: "Come out of the man, you evil spirit" (Mark 5:8, NLT).

Soon the man was completely healed and begged Jesus to permit him to come with Him.

But Jesus said, "No, go home to your family, and tell them everything the Lord has done for you and how merciful he has been" (Mark 5:19, NLT). Jesus expected him to use his tragic Egypt period and his eventual deliverance as a testimony to God's goodness and grace.

One of the great testimonies of God's grace was written by John Newton, the former captain of a slave ship. After years of working in the sad business of human trafficking, Newton came to Christ. Perhaps it was the memory of his Egypt of wretchedness that motivated him to write the hymn that begins, "Amazing grace, how sweet the sound, that saved a wretch like me. I once was lost, but now am found, was blind but now I see." Newton's wretched Egypt of transgression gave birth to an immortal song that still warms the hearts of Christians around the world.

Live with Gratitude

Remembering Egypt can fill us with a spirit of gratitude. Some people have a sense of entitlement, believing that the world owes them something. Such people often have difficulty even saying thank you. They go through life taking their blessings for granted.

This was not the case with one of the ten lepers Jesus healed in Luke 17. All ten were cleansed, but only one was a stranger, a despised Samaritan who had been drawn into a group of Jewish outcasts, all of them ostracized because of their incurable disease. Common suffering often creates bonds of friendship that elude us during good times. All ten were cleansed, but only one returned and bowed in humble gratitude before the Savior who had freed him from the prison of that dreadful disease. That one was the Samaritan. Jesus seemed disappointed with the lack of gratitude in the majority, inquiring, "Were not ten cleansed? Where are the nine?" (Luke 17:17, ESV).

Could it be that this grateful Samaritan knew the Egypt of discrimination and mistreatment? Could it be that the double stigma of disease and race made his experience of being quarantined even more painful than those of his ethnically superior colleagues? Whatever the reason, his heart overflowed with gratitude. He is an exemplary model of the gratitude that should be produced when we remember our own private Egypts.

Many years ago I was stationed in Korea and had to endure the hardships of training in the brutal cold. With temperatures below freezing, we slept on the ground and went without showers or baths for more than a month. Many times the burdens seemed more than I could bear, but by God's grace I persevered, surviving with the others. In the years since, memories of those circumstances have been a great blessing. Whenever I'm faced with challenges in my present life, I remember Korea and my heart overflows with thanksgiving for life's simple pleasures. No one can appreciate something as simple as a daily shower quite like someone who went for more than a month without one. Permit your memory of Egypt to ignite your gratitude.

Embrace Humility

The apostle Paul once asked proud Corinthian believers, "What do you have that you have not been given?" (1 Corinthians 4:7). He wanted them to forsake their pride by remembering that all talents and abilities come from above.

Remembering Egypt should create in our hearts an unfeigned humility. How can we claim to deserve special treatment when we remember the depths from which God has taken us? Perhaps one of the things that made Paul so humble was his memory of having persecuted the early Christian church. In Ephesians 3:8, Paul describes himself as less than the least of all believers, a perception most likely rooted in his checkered past. Often he would talk about how he had persecuted Christians before his Damascus road encounter with Jesus (Acts 9). His memories of his Egypt inoculated him against pride.

Learn from Failure

We often learn more from our failures than our successes; hence, remembering the Egypt of our missteps can bring us blessings. The Bible predicts that the day will come when sin will not rise a second time (Nahum 1:9). Perhaps this is the case because those who experience sin's failures see transgression with the mask of deception removed. Is there anyone who, looking back at his or her past mistakes, does not wish he or she had done the good and wholesome thing instead of the sinful and unproductive one? Joseph's brothers' memories of failure blessed them in the long run. Having fallen on hard times, they remembered their mistreatment of Joseph and felt that God was punishing them. "If we had only treated our brother better," they moaned, "God would not permit these evils to befall us" (Genesis 42:21). Remembering Egypt prepared them for reunion with their brother and a life of service and integrity.

I try to remember my failures by performing an autopsy on my mistakes. I look for the tipping point, attempting to understand where I passed the point of no return. This analysis is helpful in preventing me from making similar mistakes in the future. When the emotions are gone and the heat of the moment is a distant memory, a dispassionate understanding of what went wrong is often more easily obtained. Failure, then, becomes a teacher whose instruction will produce positive dividends for years. These dividends often take the form of victory when I encounter the same temptation again. The knowledge that I am able to overcome something that would have beaten me in the past allows me to celebrate my troubles in victory.

AN ACTION PLAN TO HELP YOU ACCEPT THE INEVITABILITY OF TROUBLE

> *Avoid resignation.*

> *Tame your temper.*

> *Find joy.*

> *Reap the fruit of perseverance.*

> *Harness the power of prayer.*

> *Ask God for wisdom.*

> *Remember the past.*

> *Help the helpless.*

> *Endure hardship.*

> *Testify to God's goodness.*

> *Live with gratitude.*

> *Embrace humility.*

> *Learn from failure.*

8

WIN BY WAITING

IT WAS AN ILLUMINATING DRIVE TO WORK. The DC traffic swarmed over the expressway leading into the nation's capital, hopelessly clogging the thoroughfare, but giving me plenty of time to listen to a Bible tape on the book of Exodus as I headed for my office in the Capitol Building. The narrator's booming voice resonated with a delightful British accent that made the listening all the more pleasant. He read Exodus 14 with such intensity that I listened to the familiar story of Israel's miraculous crossing of the Red Sea with an excitement I hadn't felt in years.

Assailed by the marauding Egyptian armies, God's people were hemmed in on both sides with no escape. And as the murderous Egyptians chased them from the rear, driving them into the raging sea, they faced seemingly insurmountable adversity.

When the speaker reached verse 13—"Fear not, stand still and see the salvation of the Lord"—my heart leapt with thanksgiving. God seemed to be challenging Israel to wait for Him to act. This was not a time to rummage desperately in their hats for rabbits to pull out; not a time for striving, fretting, or worrying. The message was clear: relax, stay calm. Stand still and wait for God to act. And though I had to keep my hands on the steering wheel, and thus was reluctant to lift them in praise to God, I began praising Him with my voice. Such a glorious and affirming declaration demanded it: Wait for God to act. Turn adversity into advantage and celebrate your troubles by learning the wisdom of waiting.

I believe victory is a part of the destiny of every child of God. This victory won't be measured from a worldly perspective, however; for what the carnal mind calls success may be failure in God's eyes. On the surface, Good Friday seemed like a failure for Jesus, but Easter Sunday shined the spotlight on His glorious victory. He rested in the tomb waiting for His Father's will, and then He arose! He practiced the wisdom of waiting.

Wait for God

The Bible is full of admonitions to wait upon the Lord. Why? Why does God so often make us wait? Why is patience and perseverance so important to Him? He could have sent Christ the day Adam and Eve fell into sin, but He delayed this redemptive act and made humanity wait for thousands of years for Bethlehem's breakthrough. God could have destroyed the Egyptian army as easily as He sent the ten plagues on Egypt. He could have caused the Egyptians' chariot wheels to come off long before the enemy soldiers pursued the Israelites into the sea. Instead, He remained silent and did not move; He made His people wait. It's fair to say that most people would have handled events differently if they had been given the chance to orchestrate a plan to deliver Israel from slavery. Why then does God, who loves us passionately, respond to us in ways that seem so inconsistent with unconditional love? Why does He make us wait?

There are no easy answers to this question and no shortcuts to godly character. But I have found through my reading of the Scriptures, and through my own experience, that God frequently uses the waiting period as an entrance exam for many of His blessings, with patience being the curve He grades us on.

Genesis 40 finds Joseph rotting in prison, the victim of a wrongful conviction. According to the account, he had just interpreted the dreams of two of his cellmates, Pharaoh's butler and baker, and God seemed finally to be moving on his behalf. Being supernaturally endowed to interpret both of these dreams must have had him brimming with the hope that it wouldn't be long before he was released from his unjust incarceration. I'll bet he was counting the days in anticipation of walking through those dungeon doors a free man.

But it didn't happen. The days gradually dragged on with no word from Pharaoh. *Surely by now the butler has talked to Pharaoh*, Joseph must have thought. The days stretched into weeks, and weeks slipped into months. The months became years. Two agonizing years crawled by before God sent Pharaoh two mysterious and disturbing dreams, the report of which nudged the butler's sluggish memory so that he finally remembered Joseph. Yet not once did Joseph complain or murmur, for his trials had taught him the wisdom of waiting. He passed God's test, proving that he was qualified for higher blessings and could be faithful with greater responsibilities. What tests has God sent your way that seem difficult to pass because they require waiting? In what ways are you failing to exhibit the patience needed for robust spiritual and ethical fitness? If, like Joseph, you learn to trust God in the dark, when you can't see clearly the road ahead, you'll often reap a harvest of great blessings.

Waiting not only tests our character but also strengthens our faith. Sometimes God delays in order to intensify our trust in Him. In John 11, as Lazarus lies dying, the Lord deliberately lingers in another town until His suffering friend has actually succumbed to his illness. Upon learning of Lazarus's death, Jesus says something very strange to His disciples: "Lazarus is dead, and for your sake I am glad I was not there, so that you may believe" (John 11:14-15, NIV).

Jesus knew His disciples would be shattered by the events surrounding His own death and burial and needed to develop a resilient faith that could endure until His resurrection. They would need a confidence strong enough to continue trusting Him when everything they saw crushed their dreams and filled them with dread. Jesus knew also that Jewish leaders and hired mourners would attend Lazarus's funeral. They needed spiritual help as well, though for different reasons than the disciples, so the Savior capitalized on this opportunity to lay a foundation for their faith. Seizing the day, Jesus practiced the wisdom of waiting with an eye to strengthening the faith of many people, preparing them for future success.

A final reason why God sometimes makes us wait is to counter our pride, delaying so that praise for the victory will go to Him and not to humanity. He challenged Gideon (Judges 7), telling him that he had too many soldiers for God to give him victory over the Midianites. He didn't want Israel to say, "Our own hand has saved us." God winnowed Gideon's army down from 32,000 to 300 soldiers, ensuring that the glory for their imminent victory could not possibly go to human prowess. He compelled Gideon's army to wait on Him. By thinning out their numbers so drastically, He stripped them of their ability to make even a dignified showing in the combat zone without supernatural aid. In His wisdom,

God placed His people in a position that made it impossible to be puffed up with pride over a well-fought battle.

Trust God's Providence

When God decrees that you must wait, bolster your patience by remembering His faithfulness and His commitment to the covenant He has sealed with His blood. He takes His promises seriously even when we don't, pledging to protect us with the shield of His favor (Psalm 5:12) if we obey His commands. So whether you're standing tall on the mountaintop of achievement or lying flat on your back in the valley of despair, as long as God is with you, you can rest in His love and count on His faithfulness. In Matthew 14, Jesus directs His disciples to sail across a lake after He has miraculously fed five thousand people. As His followers push off from the shore, the Lord climbs a nearby mountain to meet with God in a brief session of much-needed solitude and prayer. Soon, however, a fierce squall arises, and the disciples are forced to fight for their lives against the fury of a storm-tossed sea. The disciples panic until Jesus appears to them once more, walking toward their beleaguered craft across the waves. Despite their natural fears, they should have been able to peer through the ravages of the storm and see their Lord's promises, for they were exactly where Jesus had asked them to be. Why would they fear when they were doing His bidding?

The knowledge that you're following God's plan for your life should enable you to trust Him to lead you to His desired destination. When I was a boy, I was intrigued by a bus commercial that invited potential customers to "Trust Greyhound, and leave the driving to us." Being within the shelter of God's will is like being safely ensconced in a Greyhound bus: You can give up the reins of control and wait for God to act, confident that He will not disappoint you. Girded with His promises, we can shout the words of Job: "He knows the way I take; when He has tried me, I shall come forth as gold" (Job 23:10, NASB).

This is exactly what happened to three young Israelite men in exile in Babylon, who were convicted of a capital crime and sentenced to death by King Nebuchadnezzar. They were to be thrown alive into a blazing furnace (Daniel 3), which had been heated until it was seven times hotter than normal. What offense was deserving of such an extreme punishment?

Nebuchadnezzar, one of the most feared kings of his day, had commanded all his subjects to bow to an enormous gold likeness of himself that towered over the plain of Dura. This newly enacted law decreed that when certain music was played, the people were to pay homage and bend their knees to the image in an act of blatant idolatry, venerating the king as if he were a god. But the three young men had refused to bow. These three men, though exiles in a foreign land, had remained faithful to the true God. Even in the face of the king's command they had demonstrated the depth of their love for God by refusing to bend their knees to the image of a mere man. Their refusal was reported to the king, who offered them a second chance to comply with his edict. In full knowledge of the severity of the consequences for following their convictions, they chose to risk death rather than bow. Upon the second refusal, their conduct was treated as a criminal act and punished accordingly. The good news is that God rewarded their faithfulness with a dramatic deliverance.

Refuse to Murmur and Complain

Similarly, facing a violent death with the Red Sea before them and the Egyptian army breathing down their necks, the Israelites' faith and courage dissolved into a backlash of murmuring and complaining. "Didn't we have enough graves in Egypt?" they cried in desperation. "Moses, why have you brought us out here to die?" (Exodus 14:11).

Their pessimistic predictions dishonored God and demonstrated a deep lack of trust in His faithfulness. This trust deficit eventually led to their demise, as their relentless complaints became self-fulfilling prophecies. Most of the adult Israelites who escaped from Egypt never reached the Promised Land. Instead, they languished in the wilderness and eventually died there.

In the New Testament parable of the talents (Matthew 25:14-30), we can see clearly the danger of murmuring and complaining. You'll recall that in the story, three servants are given varying amounts of money—five talents to the first man, two to the second, and one to the third. The man who is given the one talent refuses to risk investing it, opting instead to bury the money. When he is called to account for his actions, he grumbles to the master, "I knew you were a hard master, reaping where you haven't sown, so I hid my talent in the earth" (Matthew 25:24-25). Judgment falls swiftly and with exacting precision, hastened by his complaint; his solitary talent is taken from him and given to his more conscientious peer.

The things we say can make or break us. As Proverbs 18:21 so aptly puts it, "The tongue has the power of life and death" (NIV). It can be hard to stay the course while waiting for God to act, and even harder to do it without questioning Him or complaining about His timetable. But given how binding the consequences of our speech can be, we should strive to emphasize the positive and eliminate the negative by repudiating the sin of murmuring.

Remember What God Has Already Done

Was it realistic to expect the Israelites not to panic or complain when facing the Red Sea with the fury of the Egyptian army at their backs? It was when you consider what God had already done for them. He had unshackled them from the bondage of slavery, visiting the nation of Egypt with ten powerful plagues until Pharaoh relented and released them. The final blow came on the night when the angel of death struck the firstborn sons in Egypt, claiming all their lives (Exodus 11). By the time the Israelites came face-to-face with the Red Sea, God had given sufficient evidence of His power for them to trust Him even when death seemed imminent.

Israel should have done what the shepherd boy David did and expressed faith instead of doubt. David based his faith on the evidence of God's mighty deeds. When he volunteered to go up against Goliath, those closest to him sought to discourage him. "You can't succeed," said King Saul, "for you're a boy and Goliath has been a warrior since his youth" (1 Samuel 17:33).

But the pessimists were no match for David's faith and idealism, and he was quick to remind the king that God had already delivered him from the paws of a lion and a bear. "This Philistine will be as one of them," he vowed. Remembering what God had already done, David was prepared to trust Him for future blessings. This same David wrote, "Bless the LORD, O my soul, and forget not all His benefits" (Psalm 103:2, NKJV). Those who practice the wisdom of waiting maintain their trust in God for the future by remembering His past actions, both in their lives and in the history of the world.

Believe God Can Do the Impossible

Sometimes we fail to wait for God to act because the challenge seems too great. We believe God can accomplish some things, but others are too difficult for Him. At these times, we're like the friend who went to Jairus, an official of the synagogue whose daughter had been desperately ill, and said, "Your daughter is dead. Why trouble the Master any longer?" (Luke 8:49). Fortunately, Jairus trusted Jesus instead, clinging to His admonition to believe, and continued to make his way in faith. Upon arriving home with Jesus, the man's faith was rewarded, for Jesus did the impossible, resurrecting his daughter.

Also in defiance of the natural order, the first chapter of the Gospel of Luke recounts the appearance of an angel to Mary with the announcement that she would supernaturally conceive and then give birth to the promised Messiah. The unassuming Jewish maiden was incredulous: "How can this be, for I have never been with a man?" she meekly asked her heavenly envoy. "Is there anything too hard for the Lord?" the angel responded. Those who wait for God to act have learned that He can do more than they can ask or imagine (Ephesians 3:20), even the impossible.

Lean on Faith, Not on Works

Waiting for God to act becomes easier when we lean on faith and not on works. Standing at the brink of the Red Sea, the children of Israel wrestled with the following command: "Stand still, and see the salvation of the LORD" (Exodus 14:13, NKJV). In other words, "Stop struggling; quit working to save yourself; trust the divine process."

The divine process is *grace*. Trying to be saved through human efforts is similar to attempting to jump the Grand Canyon. Human efforts fall pathetically short of all that is needed to reach that far. It's just not going to happen without help. Some people may be able to jump farther out than others, but in the last analysis, every attempt ends with people plunging to their death, for no one can make it over the chasm without assistance.

Ephesians 2:8 tells us that salvation comes "by grace through faith." It is freely given to us by God, enabling us to leap over the chasm, energized by faith. Where works fall short, hamstrung by human limitations that depend on the natural world and its corresponding laws, faith engages the supernatural vigor of God, enabling us to accomplish all He desires for us.

The military officer in Matthew 8 possessed this wonderful faith fuel. He came to Jesus pleading for assistance for a sick servant who was very dear to him. "I'll hurry to your home," Jesus responded.

"Oh no," responded the centurion. "Lord, You simply need to speak the words, and my servant will be healed."

Jesus was amazed and said, "I haven't found faith like this even among God's chosen people!" This Gentile soldier possessed an understanding of Christ's power that even Jesus' disciples lacked, and his faith pleased Jesus so completely that He healed the servant immediately.

Are you willing to wait for God to act? Do you have a quality of faith that believes He can and will do the impossible? Do you possess a passionate fidelity to God's promises that will enable you to stand still and see His salvation? Only then will your strength be renewed, allowing you to mount up with eagles' wings. Only then will you "run and feel no weariness, walk and not feel faint" (Isaiah 40:31).

For the life we are called to is a life that has passed *through* death, not around it. And when the crushing weight of the loads we carry drives us to our knees, we wait and rise in the power of the Cross, losing our lives that we might gain them.

AN ACTION PLAN TO HELP YOU WIN BY WAITING

> *Wait for God.*

> *Trust God's providence.*

> *Refuse to murmur and complain.*

> *Remember what God has already done.*

> *Believe God can do the impossible.*

> *Lean on faith, not on works.*

9

BRING BLESSINGS FROM PAIN

WHILE GROWING UP in Baltimore's inner city, I never dreamed that my troubles would one day be used to bless others. Even my most tragic day, the day of my mother's death, became an occasion for God to bring opportunity from a season of grief. I didn't see how good could come from the premature death of a loved one, but it did.

A few years after my mother's death, I sat with a woman who was frozen with grief, having learned of the death of her two young-adult daughters. These beautiful girls had been killed in an accident, and this mother was inconsolable. None of my words seemed to break through the fog of her agony. She lay rigid on a couch, staring vacantly. Then I began to tell her about my mother's death. "You know," I said, "I prayed some angry prayers. I told God that He didn't even have the decency to bring my mother from her coma so that I could tell her good-bye, something I would have done for an enemy!" I then talked to her about how

God managed to rescue me from my dark night of anguish, but still I received no response from this grief-stricken mother. She answered me not a word. Had she heard me? I felt I had definitely missed the mark.

An hour later, I discovered that my feeling of failure was premature. As I prepared to leave, she stood and embraced me. Almost startled by her actions, I waited for her to speak. She muttered words I had difficulty understanding, so I stooped to hear more clearly. Then I heard her say softly, but quite audibly, "What you said to me today is the only thing that has made some sense during this whole dreadful ordeal." She kissed me on the cheek as I said good-bye. Thank God. My feeble words had made a connection and brought comfort. God had permitted me to use my pain to bless someone else. A mother had been comforted with the comfort I had received from God, benefiting from the blessings I had found in my trouble.

Expect Trouble

Why do bad things happen to good people? That's a question life often forces us to ponder. I've found myself meditating on it more often than I desire. The answer sometimes seems elusive. Obviously, some suffering comes to us because we're human. In Job 14:1, the Bible reminds us that human beings live short and troubled lives. The nature of our earthly pilgrimage is challenge. To quote from Longfellow again, "Life is real! Life is earnest! *And the grave is not its goal.*"

M. Scott Peck begins his wonderful book *The Road Less Traveled* with the observation, "Life is difficult." In John 16:33, Jesus makes an ominous statement to His disciples: "In this world you will have trouble" (NIV). Are you living on planet Earth? Then you can count on troubles.

Other troubles come to us because we love and serve God. Light is an enemy to darkness, and truth is no friend of falsehood. Like oil and water, don't expect righteousness and unrighteousness to mix. Second Timothy 3:12 promises, "All those who live godly lives will suffer persecution." Don't permit troubles to surprise you; they are backhanded compliments from the enemy of our souls.

Still other trials come to us because God is glorified by our challenging predicaments, using our pain for His glory. A good example is the man who was born blind (John 9:3). His congenital predicament did not come as a result of sin, but rather "so that God's works could be revealed." This is finding benefits in affliction, when God uses what seems to be negative in our lives to reveal Himself as God or to bring positives into the lives of others.

Experience God's Grace and Peace

We prepare for God to use our pain to bless others by first experiencing His grace and peace. The apostle Paul writes: "Grace be to you and peace from God our Father, and from the Lord Jesus Christ" (2 Corinthians 1:2, kjv). The great apostle goes on to talk about how God comforts us in order to empower us to comfort others. But this empowerment is preceded by experiencing God's grace and peace. This peace gives us a calmness in the midst of life's storms and enables us to see our pain in the proper perspective. Such a perspective once enabled David to write, "Before I was afflicted I went astray: but now have I kept thy word" (Psalm 119:67, kjv).

What does this experience of grace and peace feel like? It's similar to what Elisha experienced in 2 Kings 6. At that time, the king of Syria was at war against Israel, sending soldiers to capture

God's prophet in Dothan. He sent soldiers and chariots by night, surrounding the town where Elisha dwelled. Looking out the window in the morning, the prophet's servant saw the enemy soldiers surrounding his home and cried, "Alas, my master! What shall we do?" (2 Kings 6:15, NASB).

But Elisha didn't panic. He knew the serenity of God's grace and peace and could see what his protégé couldn't. "Lord," prayed the prophet, "open the young man's eyes" (2 Kings 6:17). And when the servant's eyes were opened, he saw that the surrounding hills were full of celestial horses and chariots. Then he realized that God's provisions were greater than their needs, and this visible manifestation of God's grace gave him peace.

What disrupts your peace? What causes you to see trials as obstacles rather than as opportunities? By experiencing God's grace and peace, you'll be able to handle life's storms without fear or panic. And by praying with gratitude as you let God know what you desire, you will be imbued with a supernatural peace that defies human explanation (Philippians 4:6-7).

Begin now to pray about whatever troubles you. But as you pray, permit gratitude to give wings to your petitions, so that divine peace can flood your heart. This peace will lead you to step two—a life of praise.

Live with Praise

How often do you praise God? David said, "I will bless the LORD at all times: his praise shall continually be in my mouth. My soul shall make her boast in the LORD: the humble shall hear thereof, and be glad. O magnify the LORD with me, and let us exalt his name together" (Psalm 34:1-3, KJV). It's clear that, by the time he penned this psalm, David had learned to live a life of praise.

Why live a life of praise? It's quite simple: Our God inhabits praise (Psalm 22:3). Thanksgiving invites God's presence into our lives and our present situations. It is no accident that when Paul and Silas experienced the affliction of an unjust incarceration, they not only found comfort in singing, but they used praise to invite heaven's help. Their praise triggered the earthquake that freed them and brought spiritual liberation to their warden and his family (Acts 16). What unjust circumstances or unfair challenges are you facing? Have you been betrayed by a friend or a loved one? Has the burden of unemployment been placed on your shoulders? Has the serenity of your world been threatened by grief's dark clouds? Then don't forget to praise the Lord. No matter what your circumstances, obey the biblical injunction to give thanks, "for this is God's will for you in Christ Jesus" (1 Thessalonians 5:18, NASB).

I have found a transforming practice for my personal times of sorrow that should help you. I simply pause and make a list of all the things for which I am grateful to God. In short, I count my blessings; name them ten by twenty. Living with thankfulness invites God's presence and power, enabling us to find comfort in the midst of trials.

Bless the Lord

Did you know that you have a duty to bless the Lord? You'll find it will enable you to turn your adversity into advantage. "David said to all the assembly, 'Bless the LORD your God.' And all the assembly blessed the LORD, the God of their fathers, and bowed their heads and paid homage to the LORD" (1 Chronicles 29:20, ESV). Blessing the Lord means praising Him and giving Him the honor due His name.

Giving God appropriate honor is so important that it's expected even of nature. The psalmist writes, "Praise the LORD from the earth, ye dragons, and all deeps: Fire, and hail; snow, and vapor; stormy wind fulfilling his word: Mountains, and all hills; fruitful trees, and all cedars" (Psalm 148:7-9, KJV). Can nature really praise the Lord? Jesus seemed to think so. When some Pharisees criticized the Palm Sunday praises of the multitude, Jesus said, "If they don't give praise, the rocks will cry out" (Luke 19:40). Yes, even inanimate nature can adore its Creator. I don't want *rocks* to give God more praise than I am willing to give.

Sometimes I begin my sermons by reminding the congregation of why I'm there. I tell them that I traveled to worship not because of my ministry position, but because praise is what I do. I deeply feel the joy of praise in every worship setting and enjoy participating in the corporate worship and praise of Christ. I then tell the people that we must learn to praise God when we're not in church, for people who only engage in weekend praise are several days tardy. Praising God at all times develops your ability to bless Him in any setting. Those accustomed to this habitual praise don't need a choir or music or prayers to lift their spirits into heavenly places. They bring their praise with them to every worship venue because it's part of how they live and breathe.

Do you praise God daily, finding time for intimacy with Him? When your day begins, how long does it take you before you think about God's goodness? Do you bless the Lord at all times, with praises to Him rising continually from your lips? If you do, you're well on your way to finding blessing in your adversity.

Develop the Right Perspective

As a boy, I heard this little rhyme: "Two men looked out from behind prison bars; one saw the mud, the other saw the stars." This couplet, attributed to Frederick Langbridge, reminds me of the power of perception. It seems to echo the declaration that

Shakespeare put in the mouth of Hamlet: "There is nothing either good or bad, but thinking makes it so."

Praise affects our perception. It reminds us of God's goodness and of how He has already blessed us. Again, David says, "Bless the LORD, O my soul: and all that is within me, bless his holy name. Bless the LORD, O my soul, and forget not all his benefits" (Psalm 103:1-2, KJV). You see, when you remember the ways in which you have already benefited from God's blessings, it changes your perception of the latest trial.

One of the pleasant things I remember about my father is the way he responded to the question, "How are you?" He almost always replied, "I can't complain." With the passing of time, that response becomes more and more appropriate. For when we remember all God has done for us, how can we possibly complain?

Complaining was one of the Israelites' great mistakes on their way from Egypt to Canaan. They complained about the shortages of food and water and longed for the spicy foods they had eaten in Egypt (Numbers 20). Perhaps they forgot God's benefits. They were no longer in slavery, for God had brought them out of Egypt with a mighty hand. He had guided them with a cloud and given them water from rocks. Their shoes and clothing didn't wear out, and they had been protected from desert predators. But still they complained, and this failure to remember God's goodness kept most of them from the Promised Land.

The late, great gospel singer James Cleveland used to sing a song with the lyrics, "I don't believe God has brought me this far to leave me." What an awesome celebration of God's goodness. Cleveland was saying that he could look back over the difficult road God had already taken him down and find a reason for praise. The God who had kept him alive through sickness and setback, frustrations and failure, was still alive and well and able to continue His providential leading. This knowledge invigorated Cleveland and enabled him to remember God's blessings and benefits.

What about you? As you look back, do you see how God's providence has guided your life, even through the valleys? Are you confident that God can keep and sustain you? Have you counted your blessings and realized that your life is better than it could be? Having this perspective will remove the sting from your troubles.

Lean on the Father of Mercies

Paul calls God "the Father of mercies" (2 Corinthians 1:3). Mercy is a critical divine attribute to celebrate, for it is because of God's mercy that humanity has not been destroyed (Lamentations 3:22). God's mercy toward me causes my heart to sing ceaseless praises.

In Matthew 9:27-29, two blind men follow Jesus, begging Him for mercy. Jesus turns to them and asks a question about their faith: "Do you believe I can heal you?" When they say yes, He touches their eyes saying, "According to your faith be it unto you" (Matthew 9:29, KJV). This same Jesus told His disciples that when they saw Him, they saw God (John 14:9). Christ's life gives us a portrait of God the Father, and through Christ, we can claim this same God as our Father. The mercy that Jesus showed humanity is the same mercy we can expect from our heavenly Father now and forever.

God expects us to remember His mercies. He said to the Israelites, "Thou shalt remember all the way which the LORD thy God led thee these forty years in the wilderness, to humble thee, and to prove thee, to know what was in thine heart, whether thou wouldest keep his commandments, or no" (Deuteronomy 8:2, KJV).

Remembering God's mercies not only compels us to praise, but it also helps us resist temptation. After David sinned with Bathsheba, he was confronted by the prophet Nathan, who informed the king that God was aware of his sins and proceeded to give him a history lesson. He said, "Thus saith the LORD God of Israel, I anointed thee king over Israel, and I delivered thee out of the hand of Saul; and I gave thee thy master's house, and thy master's wives into thy bosom. . . . Wherefore hast thou despised the commandment of the LORD, to do evil in his sight?" (2 Samuel 12:7-9, KJV). God was suggesting that He had been too generous and merciful to David for him to engage in such ugly sins. Recognizing God's generous mercies will motivate us to flee from temptation and sin.

How aware are you of God's mercies in your life? Does this knowledge motivate you to want to honor Him by living a life worthy of the favor you've been given? God forbid that we should take for granted His mercies and benefits, living for ourselves rather than for His glory.

Permitting God's mercy to inspire you to right living can help you find blessings in your tough times. When your conscience is void of offense toward God and people, life's inevitable trials become all the more bearable.

Receive Divine Comfort

The great motivation necessary to bring blessings from your pain stems from a desire to emulate for the benefit of others God's willingness to comfort you in all your trials. In other words, when you want to use your own past experiences of pain to comfort others because God has comforted you, your trials are easier to bear. The apostle Paul says that God "comforts us in all our tribulation, that we may be able to comfort those who are in any trouble, with the comfort with which we ourselves are comforted by God" (2 Corinthians 1:4, NKJV).

Nothing painful can happen to you for which God cannot provide a balm, for earth has no sorrow that heaven cannot heal. Habakkuk knew this. He so rejoiced in the comfort of God's salvation that he was able to free his mind from external circumstances. In a time of testing, he declared how God's comfort had liberated him: "Although the fig tree shall not blossom, neither shall fruit be in the vines; the labor of the olive shall fail, and the fields shall yield no meat; . . . yet I will rejoice in the LORD, I will joy in the God of my salvation" (Habakkuk 3:17-18, KJV). God's salvation so comforted the prophet that he felt prepared to handle the worst that life could offer. His troubles had lost their sting.

Sometimes God sends His comfort through people in our lives. Paul writes, "God, who comforts the downcast, comforted us by the coming of Titus" (2 Corinthians 7:6, NKJV). Titus became God's vehicle of comfort for the great apostle Paul.

I met my Titus (or should I say Tituses) in the Philippines, when I was deployed to the Pacific for six months and greatly missed home. I met two sisters, Lilibeth and Eden, at a Christian Serviceman's Center, and they became God's source of comfort for me. Great cooks with many friends, they befriended me, treated me like a brother, and greatly softened my loneliness and distress. God used them as instruments of His comfort.

Have you experienced God's comfort in your life, and has it provided fuel for your praise? Have you discovered God's comfort in a developing friendship or in a companion of many years? Keep your eyes open: God is waiting to bring you comfort from above to remove the sting from your troubles, just as He did for Habakkuk.

Fulfill God's Purpose for Comfort
As you rejoice that God has brought you peace and comfort in the midst of your troubles, remember always that He comforts us

to enable us to comfort others (2 Corinthians 1:4). When Joseph was unfairly jailed, he reached out to comfort Pharaoh's butler and baker, inquiring about their well-being and the reasons for their depression (Genesis 40). The narrative account of Joseph's experience frequently states that God was with Joseph, and this abiding presence probably provided him with the comfort he needed to comfort others.

In 1968, the day before he died, Dr. Martin Luther King Jr. gave one of the great speeches of the twentieth century, "I Have Been to the Mountaintop." In this speech, he brought comfort to thousands of disenfranchised people by testifying to the comfort he had received from God. Dr. King talked about the excessive security that the airlines took to prepare for his flight from Atlanta to Memphis. He also spoke about the threats to his life that had been made by racist people. Then he went on to talk about the comfort he had received from heaven: "I just want to do God's will. And He's allowed me to go up to the mountain. And I've looked over. And I've seen the Promised Land. I may not get there with you. But I want you to know tonight, that we, as a people, will get to the Promised Land!" Thousands of African Americans took comfort because of the comfort God had given Dr. King.

Throughout America and the world, various support groups meet on a regular basis. The members of such groups are bound by a common struggle or a similar trauma. When a new member joins, that person can take comfort in the similar experiences of the others in the group.

What comfort has God given you that will enable you to help another hurting person? Were you ill and restored to health? Did God bless you to have a relationship restored? Have you faced parenting challenges that God solved? In whatever way you've been comforted by God, you are qualified to live a life of praise that will comfort others. Don't miss the opportunity.

AN ACTION PLAN TO HELP YOU BRING BLESSINGS FROM PAIN

> *Expect trouble.*

> *Experience God's grace and peace.*

> *Live with praise.*

> *Bless the Lord.*

> *Develop the right perspective.*

> *Lean on the Father of mercies.*

> *Receive divine comfort.*

> *Fulfill God's purpose for comfort.*

10

LIVE THE BLESSED LIFE

THE SONG "VIVA LA VIDA" by Coldplay was at the top of the Billboard charts for seventeen weeks. The song's instructive lyrics tell of an unsuccessful pursuit of the blessed life:

I used to rule the world.
Seas would rise when I gave the word.
Now in the morning I sleep alone,
Sweep the streets I used to own. . . .

One minute I held the key,
Next the walls were closed on me.
And I discovered that my castles stand
Upon pillars of salt and pillars of sand.[10]

Don't those words remind you of the person Jesus speaks of in Matthew 7:26-27, who seemed to have it all and yet built his house upon the sand? He possessed such power that the sea seemed to rise at his command. But, alas, he couldn't control the wind and rain, and when the sea rose up at a most inopportune time, the reality of his powerlessness flooded into his consciousness.

Is that all we can reasonably expect from life—shattered dreams and wasted years? Must all our dreams be deferred until they dry up like raisins in the sun? Must we feel for only a moment that we hold the key—to discover it was a fantasy, an illusion?

In "Bishop Blougram's Apology," the poet Robert Browning puts it this way:

> *Just when we are safest, there's a sunset-touch,*
> *A fancy from a flower-bell, some one's death,*
> *A chorus-ending from Euripides,—*

And we're lost again. It seems that optimism and beauty wait to be ambushed by life's stern and unpredictable realities. But that's not true. We can find blessings in our adversity and experience an abundant life (John 10:10). The Bible provides comprehensive principles on how to make this dream come true.

In the Sermon on the Mount (Matthew 5–7), we learn from Jesus that some of the blessed people are those with pure hearts, those who mourn, those who make peace, those who are meek, and those who are persecuted for righteousness. That's a great blueprint for finding blessing in adversity. Psalm 1 also speaks of the blessed person who ignores evil advice and meditates often upon God's Word, finding his or her delight in following biblical guidance. Do you want to live the blessed life? Let's look at some ways to reach that goal.

Know What to Ignore

Psalm 1 opens with these words: "Blessed is the man who walks not in the counsel of the ungodly" (NKJV). If you want to live the blessed life, you must learn to ignore evil counsel. Evil counsel can be heard almost everywhere you go. You hear it in the media, with suggestions about how to dress, what to drive, and how to live. Some of that counsel is beneficial, but much of it will lead you away from the biblical principles of abundant and ethical living.

Heeding the psalmist's admonition to "walk not in the counsel of the ungodly" can bring success and keep you from failure in some vital areas of your life. David provides an example of success, for he listened to Abigail's godly admonition and didn't murder her husband, Nabal, as he was determined to do. Abigail advised, "When the LORD has done all he promised and has made you leader of Israel, don't let this be a blemish on your record" (1 Samuel 25:30-31, NLT). David eventually became king without the stain of murdering Nabal on his record or conscience.

Unfortunately, David's son Amnon provides us with a tragic example of the failure that can come from following sinful counsel (2 Samuel 13). He listened to the ungodly advice of his cousin Jonadab, who advised Amnon to rape his sister, Tamar. "Pretend you're ill," Jonadab said. "And when your sister Tamar comes and prepares some food for you, you can do as you desire." Heeding this ungodly counsel cost Amnon his life, for his brother Absalom avenged the degrading and dishonoring of their sister by arranging Amnon's murder. Amnon died because he followed ungodly counsel.

In 1 Kings 12, we find the story of Rehoboam, King Solomon's son who succeeded his father on the throne of Israel. As he ascended to the crown, Rehoboam sought counsel from his father's old advisers and from some of his young friends. The older and more experienced advisers gave him good counsel: "You should strive to serve the people," they said. "If you do, the people will serve you and your kingdom will endure" (1 Kings 12:7).

But his younger advisers provided him with evil counsel: "Be sterner than even your father was, for the people need to know who's the boss" (1 Kings 12:10-11). Unfortunately, the young king followed this evil counsel. Because of his decision, he suffered catastrophic consequences. The people revolted, leaving him as ruler of only two of the original twelve tribes of Israel.

To whom do you listen and from whom do you take your cues? Do you cherish biblical counsel more than the assertions of secular experts? God's Word must be the standard by which you test your ideas and the counsel you receive from others. The prophet Isaiah put it this way: "To the law and to the testimony: if they speak not according to this word, it is because there is no light in them" (Isaiah 8:20, KJV). Test all advice and opinion by the law and testimony of Scripture to discern whether it comes from light or darkness.

Say No to Sinners
To live the blessed life, you must learn to say no to sinners. Proverbs 1:10 states: "My son, if sinners entice you, do not consent" (NKJV). This simple Bible verse saved my life during my early teenage years when I refused to follow two friends who eventually murdered someone. The same morning I memorized this verse, I refused to go with them. The refusal kept me from going to jail for life—the penalty they received for the crime. God's warnings are designed to protect us, not to destroy our joy. He challenges us to refuse to follow sinners.

Samson's life would have been more positive had he obeyed this biblical command, but he didn't. He thought he could handle Delilah, and his arrogance ruined him (Judges 16). Like Samson, we sometimes overestimate our ability to resist temptation. First Corinthians 10:12 warns, "Let those who think they stand take heed lest they fall." One of our best protections against sin is a wholesome distrust of our ability to conquer temptation.

In my effort to stay ethically fit, I've found it helpful to remember three prerequisites for moral failure: *temptation*, *desire*, and *opportunity*. These three factors are like chemicals that are harmless apart but combine to form a deadly explosive. It is easy to lose the battle against temptation when it is joined with desire and given opportunity. But when we learn to limit opportunity, desire, and temptation, keeping these combustible influences from combining, we can stay spiritually safe.

Live with Reverence

"The fear of the LORD is the beginning of knowledge, but fools despise wisdom and discipline" (Proverbs 1:7, NIV). This is the Bible's gentle reminder that we should live with *reverence*, an important attitude for the blessed life. Reverence means honoring God in the full knowledge that He is worthy of such honor. Angels seem to live with instinctive reverence for their Creator. Isaiah 6 records that in heaven there are six-winged angels called seraphim. These angels fly with two wings and cover their faces and feet with the other four. They worship God around His smoke-encircled throne, singing, "Holy, holy, holy is the LORD of hosts. The whole earth is full of His glory!" (verse 3, NKJV). That's the reverence these powerful beings have for God.

How unfortunate that people are often disrespectful to the sovereign Creator of the universe. We call Him "the man upstairs" and other casual and disparaging names, forgetting that He is the one from whom we borrow our daily ration of heartbeats. When we live with reverence, we will be humble before God, as Moses was at the burning bush (Exodus 3). He was told, "Take off your shoes, for the place on which you stand is holy ground."

A few days ago, I attended a program in the U.S. Capitol Rotunda. The program began with the parading of colors by military honor guards. As the American flag was brought into the room, hundreds of people placed their right hands over their hearts, showing respect for the flag. I can't help but notice that we often show more reverence for man-made institutions during patriotic moments than we do for spiritual things. We must learn to show an even greater reverence for God. A critical part of this reverence involves avoiding willful or premeditated sin. In Psalm 19:13, David prays, "Deliver Your servant from presumptuous sins." These are the kind of sins that we plan, the kind that have a logistical component. Because opportunity is not immediately present, we scheme to *create* an opportunity to commit the sins we desire, instead of fleeing from temptation. When we sin deliberately, we place ourselves on dangerous ground. We're like Eli's sons, who received God's fierce judgment, dying together on the same day, because of their flagrant and willful disobedience (1 Samuel 2).

Delight in God's Word

Living the blessed life is also connected to finding joy in God's Word. This ability is an acquired taste that requires us to move from discipline to delight. The discipline starts with finding a version of Scripture we enjoy—for many, this will be a contemporary translation—and reading it daily. Reading the Bible is an essential discipline, following the model of Jesus' prayer in Matthew 6, "Give us this day our daily bread." His petition didn't refer just to daily *physical* food. We must remember to receive our daily *spiritual* nourishment as well. My experience has been that continuing this daily discipline leads to delighting in God's Word.

The process of learning to love God's Word reminds me of my

boyhood war on vegetables. During my early years, I hated several vegetables, particularly squash. In spite of my mother's efforts to camouflage her squash with cheese or noodles, I would spot its distinctive flavor and protest. I made a private vow that when I became an adult, squash would cease to be a part of my meals. But something happened on my journey to adulthood. I actually began to enjoy squash, moving from distaste to delight. Like God's Word, squash for me was an acquired taste.

During my twenty-seven years in the U.S. Navy, I received many love letters from my wife when we were separated by my deployments. Like the other sailors, I read and reread the letters that came to me on board the ship, even memorizing selected sections. God's Word is a love letter to us from our Creator. We should treat it with similar respect and passion.

One way to respect God's Word is by meditating on it. The Hebrew word for *meditate* carries with it the idea of muttering. We've all at times muttered something under our breath—often things we wish later we hadn't said. I mutter things in rush-hour traffic that I'm glad no one else has the opportunity to hear. But I've learned to replace some of my instinctive muttering outbursts with Bible verses. That's right: Quoting Scripture under my breath is an effective weapon against impulsive and inappropriate speech and behavior. Speaking the verses aloud helps them to sink into my consciousness, so they become as much a part of me as my wife's letters did years ago. Redemptive muttering is a tactic that will enable you to find delight in God's Word.

Respect Life's Seasons

Do you respect life's seasons? Those who live the blessed life do. They avoid the mistake of waiting for the perfect time to be productive. Ecclesiastes 11:4 frames the challenge this way: "Those who watch the wind will not plant; those who watch the clouds will not reap." This interesting verse teaches us to respect the inevitability of seedtime and harvest (Genesis 8:22) so that we won't disrespect life's seasons. Particularly when you're young, you have a planting season. This is one of the times when you should be planting seeds for a physical, social, mental, and spiritual harvest. Things you study in your youth may prove to be invaluable for later success.

During my interview for the job of U.S. Senate Chaplain, I spent two hours answering questions from the Senate Majority Leader. He asked questions that forced me to draw on what I'd read and experienced, reaping a harvest from seeds I'd sown in my youth. Thankfully, I had made choices as a young man that enabled me to depend on such a harvest.

One of my biblical heroes is Daniel. Like me, Daniel had a government career for many decades. He'd been faithful for many years when his enemies orchestrated events that led to his being thrown into the lion's den (Daniel 6). Fortunately, he had planted seeds of faithfulness to God in his youth when he refused to defile himself with the king's food and drink (Daniel 1). Daniel respected life's seasons and earned divine rescue from the mouths of the lions.

What about you? Do you respect life's seasons? Are you starting to plan now for your future? If you're investing in your spiritual, intellectual, social, and physical growth, you're respecting life's seasons, and it will lead to a blessed life. Part of respecting the seasons entails remembering that you can't cram on a farm. In other words, you can't skip planting time and hope to make up for it by seeding the ground a few weeks before harvest. Like a farmer, you must learn to plant in the proper season so that you can reap when you should reap.

Stay Productive

Living the blessed life involves staying productive. The first command God gave to Adam and Eve was "be fruitful" (Genesis 1:28). God expects us to be productive, to be problem solvers and bearers of fruit. As Jesus put it, "Just as you can identify a tree by its fruit, so you can identify people by their actions" (Matthew 7:20, NLT).

How do we bear fruit? The parable of the talents (Matthew 25:14-30) is instructive. In this parable, the productive servants were the ones willing to take judicious risks. How does judicious risk differ from foolish risk? Judicious risk entails taking a chance while not doing anything contrary to biblical principles. For example, Peter stepped out of a good boat to walk on water (Matthew 14:22-36). It was a judicious risk because Jesus gave him permission to leave the boat and attempt the seemingly impossible. He was simply following Jesus' command. You'll be productive as well when you permit God's plan for your life to get you out of your comfort zone. After all, you'll never walk on water if you don't step out of the boat.

Receive God's Promised Success

One reason why it's easier to live the blessed life than most people think is that God promises us success. Speaking of those who daily expose themselves to God's Word and ignore evil counsel, the Bible states, "They are like trees growing beside a stream. . . . Those people succeed in everything they do" (Psalm 1:3). Isn't that awesome? You belong to a group of people who succeed in everything they do. Note that this verse doesn't say you'll succeed in everything you plan. God blesses what you do.

After Moses' death, God gave encouragement to Moses' successor, Joshua. He told the anxious Joshua to meditate on Scripture day and night, obeying what he learned. God continued: "Then you will make your way prosperous and . . . have good success" (Joshua 1:8, NKJV). Your success is really that simple. You must become a doer rather than a mere hearer of God's Word (James 1:22).

How do you know when you're experiencing success? Success comes when you fulfill God's purpose for your life. I think Billy Graham is a superb example of this kind of success. As I mentioned before, this wonderful preacher has a record of unprecedented faithfulness and is now in his tenth decade of life. During his lengthy service to God and country, not a single hint of unethical behavior has been associated with Graham's name. He's a wonderful example of a fruitful, successful servant of God.

Expect a Bright Future

God's providence provides the key to the blessed life for all who love Him. Romans 8:28 reminds us of this fact: "In everything God is working for the good for those who love Him and are called according to His purposes." This is why, as a Christian, you can give thanks in every situation (1 Thessalonians 5:18), because God's providence will transform life's negatives into positives, enabling you to experience God's best.

And what is God's best for you? It will be revealed when you look back over your life and understand how God has ordered your steps. When this happens, you can say with Joseph, "They meant it for evil, but God meant it for good" (Genesis 50:20). Isn't that amazing? Joseph looked back over his life and implied that he wouldn't change all the negative circumstances because God had worked them together for His glory and for the well-being of His servant and thousands of others. In retrospect, Joseph would have chosen the pit, the auction block, the slavery, the unfair rape charges, the cruel incarceration, and even the forgetful butler because God used these apparent setbacks for good.

No negative thing can happen in your life that God can't turn into a positive. Look at the lives of biblical heroes and heroines and notice how they came to a desired end: Abraham, Esther, Joseph, Ruth, Elijah, Elisha, and the list goes on. These people came to see that God does greater things than we can ask or imagine, according to His power working in and through us (Ephesians 3:20). Ultimately it's possible for us to live the blessed life because God turns even the worst situations into blessings for those who love Him.

AN ACTION PLAN TO HELP YOU LIVE THE BLESSED LIFE

> *Know what to ignore.*

> *Say no to sinners.*

> *Live with reverence.*

> *Delight in God's Word.*

> *Respect life's seasons.*

> *Stay productive.*

> *Receive God's promised success.*

> *Expect a bright future.*

11

FACE LIFE'S PRESSURES
WITH FAITH

I COULDN'T STAND IT. Once again, no one wanted to select me for their team in this inner-city basketball game. In fact, I was usually the last one selected during pickup games, and then it was done grudgingly and of necessity.

"I've got Bill," one team captain would say.

"Give me Larry," the other would respond.

"Then I'll take Phil." And on and on it would go, until no one was left but me and the boy with crutches.

"Well, I'll take the guy with the crutches," one of the two captains would say triumphantly, elated that the ebb and flow of the selection process had relieved him of the burden of having me on his team.

Then, with resignation and fatalism, the other boy would utter the depressing words, "All right, I guess I'll have to take Barry."

Were my basketball skills really that deficient? If so, I was determined to rectify the situation with hard work. I was convinced that diligence would pay off. I had recently memorized a Longfellow poem about work being the path to greatness:

> *The heights by great men reached and kept*
> *Were not obtained by sudden flight;*
> *But they, while their companions slept,*
> *Were toiling upward in the night.*

If the poet was right and I worked hard, I would eventually earn the respect of my peers.

I began to implement my plan. After sunset, by the eerie light of a distant streetlamp, I practiced shooting a basketball until exhaustion stopped me. Night after night, my labors continued, until I could hit nine of ten shots from twenty feet away. Elation swept over my spirit; now I was ready. *Once the guys on the playground see my freshly honed ability, I'll never be the last pick again*, I thought, almost salivating at the prospect. But soon I would painfully learn the difference between practice and a real game.

I greeted the day of my talent's unveiling with eager anticipation. In the preliminary shootaround, I demonstrated enough prowess to be the third person selected, an unprecedented event. But my faith in my hard-won abilities faltered under the pressure of a real game. When I released my newly patented set shot from twenty feet away, my opponent's hand was in my face, and this made quite a difference. To my surprise, my shooting was not nearly as accurate when someone was pressuring me with an aggressive defense. When my talents were put to the test, the harvest was less than bountiful.

What a fitting metaphor for life. Often we live and labor under practice conditions. The sun is shining, and all seems right with the world. We work a fulfilling job, and our family seems to prosper.

But then game time arrives. We lose our job, or the doctor gives us bad news. We face parenting and relationship challenges, or our nation is suddenly confronted with an unexpected crisis. "These are the times that try men's souls," wrote Thomas Paine. And so they are. They are times when our resolve is tested, and we must learn to keep our faith though pressed by many a foe. Can you keep your faith under pressure?

John the Baptist is one who had to learn to survive challenges to his faith. When the man who had announced Jesus as the Messiah found himself incarcerated by King Herod, he felt a gnawing doubt and began to question his certainty about Jesus. Finally, filled with despair, he sent his disciples to Christ with a question: "Are You the Messiah, or should we be looking for someone else?" (Luke 7:20).

Jesus seemed to realize that John's faith was being pressured. He didn't immediately respond to John's urgent query, but permitted the messengers to follow Him about and watch Him work. As the sun set, Jesus turned to John's emissaries and said, "Go tell John what you have seen and heard here today. The blind see; the lame leap; the captives are delivered" (Luke 7:21-23). This faith-filled response from Christ fortified John's spirit, enabling him to maintain his faith under pressure.

Later, Peter would have a similar test of his faith. As Jesus headed to Calvary, Peter declared his willingness to die for Christ. "Lord," he said, "I am willing to go to prison and even to die for You." Jesus surprised Peter with His response. "Simon, Simon," He said, "the devil wants to have you to sift you like wheat. But I'm praying for you, Simon, that your faith will not fail. And when you're converted, strengthen your brothers and sisters" (Luke 22:31-33).

Peter, startled by this response, continued to insist that nothing could shake his fidelity. He seemed confident that he could maintain his poise under pressure, but Jesus knew better. The Savior said, "Before the cock crows twice, you will deny Me three times" (Mark 14:30). In other words, "You will fail to keep your faith when placed under pressure." A few hours later, Jesus' prophecy came true, as Peter denied the Lord three times in the courtyard of Caiaphas the high priest (Luke 22:54-64).

Life has a way of pushing us out of our comfort zones. When I was in tenth grade, I was forced to experience the embarrassment of another eviction. I've already mentioned the feelings of shame I experienced as neighbors surveyed our poverty on full display. Being evicted pressured my faith and caused me to question God's goodness. My mother was a devoted Christian, who led her five children twice daily in family worship. She took us to church every time there was a service to attend. She sacrificed to ensure that my siblings and I matriculated at Christian schools. Could not the God she served with such faithfulness have prevented us from experiencing this public embarrassment? *God has some explaining to do*, I found myself musing.

I didn't keep my faith under pressure. When it was tested, I buckled under the strain. In John 16, Jesus seeks to prepare His disciples for the coming pressure that will confront their faith. But even as He tells them about the persecution and problems they will face, He also reminds them that He will send them a Helper, the Holy Spirit, to walk with them. Then He says, "I've told you these things that you might have peace. In this world you will have pressure. Take courage, for I have overcome the world" (John 16:33). In this simple verse, Jesus teaches us how to keep our faith under pressure.

Remain Independent of Your Circumstances

How independent are you of your external circumstances? When people say things like, "She made me angry, or upset, or depressed," they seem to be suggesting a lack of control over their own emotions. Someone *made* them feel this way. But our circumstances do not define who we are or how we must respond. We can learn to remain independent of our circumstances and live by faith, not by sight (2 Corinthians 5:7).

The Shunammite woman in 2 Kings 4:8-37 helps us to see how we can keep our attitudes and emotions independent of our environmental challenges. She had been blessed by God with a child; but when the lad grew up, he died. The mother faced this sorrow by having her son's body carried to the bedroom of the prophet Elisha, who occasionally stayed in her home. Then she rode her donkey to see the prophet, who, upon recognizing her at a distance, sent his servant to inquire, "Is it well with you? Is it well with your husband? Is it well with the child?"

How would you have answered those questions? Your son lies dead on the prophet's bed in your home, and Elisha wants to know if things are going well. Amazingly, she responded, "It is well!" In order to keep your faith under pressure like this woman, you must remain independent of external circumstances.

Jesus wanted His disciples to experience such independence. He told them that He spoke to them to give them His peace. This peace is characterized by an emotional and spiritual independence from the external world. In Philippians 4:12, the apostle Paul describes this peace: "I know both how to be abased, and I know how to abound" (KJV). In short, he had mastered his circumstances rather than permitting his circumstances to master him—he had learned to feel as comfortable with little as he did with much. Philippians 4:6-7 tells us how to maintain this independence: "Have no anxiety about anything, but pray about everything with thanksgiving. And the peace of God that passes understanding will guard your heart and mind in Christ Jesus." Whenever a concern bothers me, I capture it with grateful prayer, believing that God can solve any problem. I've discovered that when I trust God, His peace replaces my anxiety, allowing me to more easily bear the weight of life's burdens.

Expect Pressure

When we expect tribulation and pressure, as Jesus advised, they become easier to endure. One morning I decided to jog a new route in my neighborhood. As I turned a corner, the fierce sound of a barking dog pushed adrenaline through my veins. I looked around, not knowing what to expect, but visualizing a rabid pit bull. Instead I saw a small dog running along a fenced yard, powerless to do me any harm. On subsequent runs through that neighborhood, I have been ready to meet my canine friend when I turn that corner. He still barks ferociously and runs the length of the fenced yard, but I fear no evil because I expect him.

Similarly, Christians should expect pressure and trials, for Jesus declared, "Beware when all men speak well of you" (Luke 6:26). The apostle Paul cautions that "all who live godly lives will suffer persecution" (2 Timothy 3:12). And Job 14:1 makes it clear that humanity is frail, and life is short and full of trouble. In 1 Corinthians 10:13 we're told that the testing we face is common to humanity. Therefore, the ethically observant person will not go through life unscathed.

Growing up in Baltimore, my siblings and I used to hide in our home, jumping out in the darkness and shouting, "Boo!" in an effort to frighten an unsuspecting brother or sister. This game was played so often that those of us who had been frightened rarely approached a dark corner in the house without expecting someone to attempt to surprise us with a shout. That anticipation destroyed the effect. In the same way, the expectation of pressures goes a long way toward neutralizing their power to harm us or shake our faith.

Face Life's Pressure with Courage

After Jesus informed His disciples that He wanted them to experience peace by learning to expect pressures, He reminded them that they should face these pressures with courage. He wanted them to be so independent of their circumstances that they could aggressively confront and leap over the obstacles in their paths. "Take courage," He said; "I have overcome the world" (John 16:33, NASB).

The Bible is filled with examples of people who courageously handled pressure-filled challenges. Moses dealt with the arduous challenge of leading more than a million people from Egyptian slavery to the Promised Land (Exodus 3). Gideon faced armies from three nations with only three hundred men (Judges 7). Nehemiah rebuilt Jerusalem's walls in fifty-two days, despite great opposition and dangers (Nehemiah 6). David refused to be intimidated by the arrogant rhetoric of the giant Goliath (1 Samuel 17), and King Hezekiah refused to back down from the threats of the Assyrian King Sennacherib (2 Kings 18). Throughout Scripture, we find examples of faithful men and women meeting life's pressures with courage.

Where is your courage when you face pressure? Do you trust God when you receive bad news from the doctor, or your child wanders into sin's far country, or your marriage totters on the brink of ruin? None of these are easy situations to face, nor can we handle them in our own strength. Nevertheless, God expects us to approach such difficulties with courage.

Claim Your Victory

Our courage in meeting challenges is not intended to be a hopeless courage like that of a soldier making a last stand. Rather, it is the courage of one whose Master has already won the victory.

In professional football, players and fans sometimes begin to celebrate before the game is over. As the clock ticks down, players on the team that is leading pour Gatorade on their coach, congratulating him for the victory. One television football commentator used to sing, "Turn out the lights, the party's over," before the game was won, so certain was he of the outcome. Jesus wants His disciples to possess such certainty regarding His victory. It is worth repeating His words from the previous section: "Take courage; I have overcome the world." When facing life's pressures, we should rejoice in the victory that Christ has already won.

How did He win this victory? Hebrews 4:15 says, "In all points He was tempted like we are, yet without sin." Jesus absorbed the worst the devil could throw at Him and emerged more than a conqueror. On a hill called Calvary, He fully paid the sin debt of the world—reason enough for us to rejoice throughout eternity.

One of my favorite things to do is to watch recordings of pressure-filled basketball games after I know my team has already won. I watch the ebb and flow of offense and defense with the certain knowledge of how the game will end.

Likewise, I can now face life's pressures because I know how the game will ultimately end. Jesus paid the price for victory for all humankind.

Endure to the End

In high school, I participated in a track meet that taught me a valuable lesson. I ran the fastest times in two preliminary heats of the 100-yard dash, but then came the finals. In the deciding race, I leaped out ahead of the field. But just before I crossed the finish line, I looked back to see who was closest to me—and watched as my roommate beat me at the tape. Interestingly, his winning time was slower than what I had run in my previous heats. But he won because I failed to endure to the end.

To successfully face life's pressures, we must endure to the end by staying united with Christ. We must avoid the mistake of Demas, who forsook the apostle Paul, preferring instead to embrace the ways of the world (2 Timothy 4:10). Second Peter 2 warns us that we can fall away after knowing the path of righteousness. Don't get close to the finish line and then lose the race, for only "those who endure to the end will be saved" (Matthew 24:13).

Maintain the Proper Perspective

We need the correct perspective if we're to face our pressures with faith. Jesus gives one of the best blueprints in Matthew 16:24: "Any who would come after Me must deny themselves, take up their cross, and follow Me." This provides us with the correct perspective on challenges and pressures. They constitute the cross we must take up if we are to walk in Jesus' footsteps.

In this verse Jesus also tells us to forfeit our personal ambitions. We must deny ourselves and be willing, if necessary, to walk the road of sorrow and suffering. The rich young ruler in Luke 18 had to learn this outlook. He came to Jesus with the words, "Good Teacher, what must I do to inherit eternal life?" (Luke 18:18, ESV). He wanted what Jesus had to offer, but was unwilling to pay the price.

"Keep the commandments," Jesus responded (Luke 18:20).

"I have kept those since I was a youth," the man said proudly (Luke 18:21).

"Then go and sell what you have, give it to the poor, and come and follow Me," said Jesus (Luke 18:22).

This was more than the young man was willing to sacrifice. With sorrow in his heart, he walked away from Jesus, perhaps never to return. Who knows what his life could have been? Had he been willing to forfeit his personal ambitions, submitting them to Jesus' desires, he might have accomplished what the apostle Paul was able to do. God may have used him, as He did Paul, to write most of the New Testament. But he didn't have the proper perspective.

We must bear pressures, challenges, and sorrows in our lives because Christ our Savior bore them. We honor Him by carrying crosses such as the ones He carried—humility, persecution, misunderstanding, hardship, testing. And if we are faithful in meeting pressures with faith and courage, secure in the knowledge that Jesus has already won the victory, then we'll be able to find blessings in our adversity and celebrate our troubles.

AN ACTION PLAN TO HELP YOU FACE LIFE'S PRESSURES WITH FAITH

> *Remain independent of your circumstances.*

> *Expect pressure.*

> *Face life's pressure with courage.*

> *Claim your victory.*

> *Endure to the end.*

> *Maintain the proper perspective.*

12

DEAL WITH GOD'S SILENCE

HAVE YOU EVER SUSPECTED that you've misunderstood something God said in His Word? Perhaps this is how Mary and Martha felt. They had sent a message to Jesus that their brother, Lazarus, was sick. Jesus had given a wonderful response, "This sickness is not unto death" (John 11:4, KJV), but then Lazarus died—and Jesus didn't even come to the funeral. For four days, He stayed away and said nothing while the sisters had to deal with His silence and their own grief.

Have you ever wondered why God is often silent? Sometimes He's silent because of our sins that separate us from Him (Isaiah 59:1-2). At other times, He's silent because we're unprepared to hear Him. We're like Samuel, who thought he heard Eli the priest when it was God who was speaking to him. At other times, our lack of faith blocks us from hearing Him. And sometimes we don't hear His voice because of our selfishness (James 4:3).

Don't Panic

Many Bible characters experienced God's silence at one time or another. After God told Abraham to offer Isaac as a sacrifice, the patriarch confronted days of divine silence as he made his way with Isaac to the appointed place. Then God spoke again and kept him from killing his child (Genesis 22).

Think of the many years that Joseph languished as an Egyptian slave and in prison. Surely he must have cried out to God repeatedly, but God apparently said nothing. His descendants, the Israelites, cried out to God for centuries as they faced the pharaohs' cruel violence, and yet God said nothing (Exodus 2:23).

What about Gideon, in Judges 6, threshing grain in a winepress for fear of enemy soldiers? When God appeared to him, calling him a mighty man of valor, Gideon protested, "If God is with us, why are all these bad things happening to our nation?" The leader of Israel questioned God's apparent absence, for too many questions had gone unanswered for him to believe that God was still with them.

Even Jesus encountered His Father's silence. Crying out from the cross, "My God, My God, why have You forsaken Me?" (Matthew 27:46), He received no answer to His piteous cry.

And what about the tentmaker from Tarsus with the thorn in his flesh, who three times cried out to God for relief (2 Corinthians 12)? Although this great apostle wrote most of the New Testament, he had to deal with God's silence. Eventually, God broke His silence, reassuring Paul of the sufficiency of His grace (2 Corinthians 12:9).

After retiring from the U.S. Navy, I received three job offers, two of which were quite attractive. For nine months, I sought God's guidance. Which job should I take? Yet God said nothing. I waited for His peace to guide me, but felt only agitation of spirit.

For months, I experienced the frustration of needing to hear from heaven and encountering only God's silence.

What about you? Have you cried out to God and been met with only silence? If you're going to discover the blessing in your adversity, you must learn how to deal with a Savior and Lord who is sometimes silent. You must develop the ability not to panic when God says nothing and to believe that He's listening even when you sense no response.

The people I've mentioned—Abraham, Joseph, the nation of Israel, Gideon, Jesus, and Paul—all encountered God's silence. They learned, however, how to deal with this silence and reap a bountiful harvest of blessings by trusting God even when He seemed indifferent to their plight. It was often when they least expected it that God came through, speaking in clarion tones that they could hear and appreciate. They reaped a reward by patiently waiting through God's silences.

Weather the Seasons of Distress and Grief

We can encounter God's silence in any of life's seasons, for we face an unpredictable enemy, wrestling not against flesh and blood, but against spiritual wickedness in high places (Ephesians 6:12). Sometimes the silent season comes in our childhood, as it did for the boy Samuel (1 Samuel 3). After Hannah, his mother, dedicated him to the Lord, Samuel went to live with Eli the priest. As Samuel approached his teenage years, God broke His silence and spoke to him. Samuel thought it was Eli talking. He had to be taught how to listen and respond to God.

King Saul was in midlife when he dealt with God's silence. After Samuel the prophet had died, the king needed to hear from God. But God was silent, not answering him even when Saul used the techniques of the priests in the Temple to hear from heaven.

Finally Saul sought out the witch of Endor to raise up the spirit of Samuel for him to question (1 Samuel 28), so desperate was he to break God's silence.

Sometimes we encounter God's silence even during the evening of life. For more than thirty years, my mother prayed for my alcoholic father, and God said nothing. As we were growing up, she encouraged my siblings and me to continue to pray for Daddy. I did, but eventually I became discouraged. My father continued to abuse liquor, and God seemed silent. But my mother continued to pray. Then, in the evening of her life, God broke His silence and worked what seemed to us a miracle, transforming my father and freeing him from his addiction. He died a Christian.

What season of life are you in? Are you a youngster needing divine guidance, but heaven seems to give no direction? Are you in midlife, trying to navigate the difficult challenges of a promising career, but can't seem to hear God speaking? Or maybe you're in life's evening, growing somewhat cynical because of the monotonous ebb and flow of countless sunrises and sunsets, while knowing that your fondest dreams will never come true. No matter in which season of challenge you find yourself, you can deal with God's silence with patience, perseverance, and faith.

Keep Hoping and Praying

Those most likely to experience God's silence are those whom God is testing. Like giving an entrance exam for a higher level of academic accomplishment, God often tests His children before bringing them uncommon blessings. Before Joseph became Egypt's prime minister, he had to wait for two more years in prison after helping Pharaoh's men. God said nothing, but Joseph didn't murmur or complain. And when God spoke, He did so with great efficacy, moving His servant from prison to power in less than twenty-four hours.

Moses, a fugitive from justice, had a similar experience. For forty years, he fled from the law, tending his father-in-law's sheep in the wilderness of Midian. Day after day and year after year he did this monotonous work, and God said nothing. But one day, this leader in exile encountered an ever-burning-yet-never-burned bush, and out of the midst of it he heard God speak. God informed him of a great blessing. In spite of his criminal past, Moses had been chosen to lead God's people out of Egypt's chains to the Promised Land's freedom.

During the civil rights movement in Alabama in the 1950s, African American citizens initiated a bus boycott. They did this to protest the segregated conditions on public transportation, and they encountered fierce resistance from those interested in protecting the status quo. For more than a year, they walked rather than endure the humiliation of riding without dignity. They cried out to God, but the opposition seemed to be winning, and heaven offered no solace. When it seemed that all was lost and their enemies had won, they received a great blessing. The U.S. Supreme Court ruled in their favor. The months of divine silence turned out to be the prelude to great blessings.

Could it be that God's silence in your life simply means you're a candidate for future blessing? If so, your attitude may determine if you'll pass or fail His test. By refusing to second-guess Him or to express doubts regarding God's goodness, you may be preparing yourself to receive double for your trouble. Keep hoping and praying.

Find Answers in God's Word
Sometimes God keeps silent to bring forth our faith. We see an example of this with the Gentile woman in Matthew 15. This woman passionately sought Jesus' help because a demon possessed

her daughter. She expressed her anguish to Jesus, and the Bible records, "He answered her not a word" (Matthew 15:23, NKJV). Jesus didn't say yes or no, or even wait; He uttered not a single syllable. When Jesus finally did speak, it was not to the woman. He spoke to His disciples, informing them that He had been sent only to the lost sheep of Israel, not to the Gentiles at that time. But the woman continued to cry out to Him, even though He seemed to ignore her plea. At last He spoke to her, but it was with words that must have been difficult for her to understand: "It is not right for Me to take the children's food and give it to the dogs" (Matthew 15:26). Whoa! Wait just one minute, Jesus. Aren't You insulting this woman?

Whatever He meant, this woman seemed to sense a method to His silence and His apparent insult. With great faith, she responded to the challenge: "Yes, Lord, but even the puppies are permitted to eat the crumbs that fall from their master's table" (Matthew 15:27).

Jesus smiled and responded, "Woman, you have great faith! Your request is granted" (Matthew 15:28). Her daughter was healed at that very hour. This woman's willingness to persevere helped her deal with God's silence.

How did this woman get Jesus to break His silence? First, she came to Him with love as her motivation. She wasn't coming for herself, but for her daughter. We should learn from her example to let love motivate our prayers and to pray less selfishly. Second, she knew Jesus was listening even when He didn't speak. God hears your cries even when He's silent. Third, she didn't blame herself. God's silence may have little to do with us. Once, after Daniel waited three weeks to hear from God, an angel finally showed up. He told Daniel, "God heard you when you first prayed, but I had to do battle with the Prince of the Kingdom of Persia on my way to you" (Daniel 10:12-13). Daniel had nothing to do with this delay. Fourth, the Gentile woman found answers in Christ's words. Though He didn't speak directly to her at first, she listened to what He said to His disciples and gleaned hope from it. She then listened carefully to what He said to her about feeding dogs and used His statement to demonstrate her faith to Him. When God is silent in your life, find answers in His Word.

Hold On to God's Promises
One of the best ways to persevere during times of God's silence is to read His promises and claim them. Cling to what He has promised to do for His children, knowing that He keeps His word and would never lie.

Eventually, the Gentile woman broke through God's silence by perseverance. Are you willing to persevere in prayer when God is silent? Elijah in 1 Kings 18 prayed for God to send fire to consume the sacrifice on Mount Carmel and received an immediate response. That's wonderful. It was not so wonderful later in the chapter, when he prayed for rain and God said nothing. But he persevered, praying seven times before he received a small hint that God was listening. When God says nothing, persevere until He speaks. Persist in prayer until God responds.

AN ACTION PLAN TO HELP YOU DEAL WITH GOD'S SILENCE

> *Don't panic.*

> *Weather the seasons of distress and grief.*

> *Keep hoping and praying.*

> *Find answers in God's Word.*

> *Hold on to God's promises.*

13

USE IT OR LOSE IT

THE NEW U.S. SENATOR was petite and attractive. Our eyes fixed on her as she stood to speak at the Senate's weekly prayer breakfast, an opportunity for senators to forge friendships and to learn about their colleagues' individual faith journeys. She spoke with the distinct accent of her home state, articulating her story with confidence, power, and persuasiveness. In spite of the fact that she seemed almost too young to be a senator, her words compelled us to listen. She said, "I've found in two Christian parables great guidance and strength—the stories of the talents and of the farmer recorded in Matthew 25 and 13 respectively. These stories have been a lamp for my feet and a light for my path."

After her wonderful presentation, I took the elevator to my office in the U.S. Capitol Building, eager to read again these wonderful stories. Entering my office, I picked up a contemporary translation of the Bible and turned to the two passages. They came alive as I remembered some of the points the senator had made.

I read first the story of the talents, then the story of the farmer. This prompted me to look at a third story, in John 6, the feeding of the five thousand. I saw a common theme of "use it or lose it" in these three stories, particularly in the third one when Jesus said, "Gather up the fragments; don't waste the leftovers" (John 6:12). Then I flipped back to the story of the talents in Matthew 25, continuing my meditation.

The story of the talents is about a man who gave talents (a unit of money) to his servants before leaving on a long journey. On the surface, the distribution seemed unfair, for one received five talents, another two, and the third servant only one. The master left, expecting that his servants would invest his money and show a profit when he returned. The months flew by, and soon the boss returned to inquire what the workers had accomplished. The first two, who had each doubled their money, received from their pleased employer grateful words of appreciation. But the one with the single talent was less fortunate. He had not invested the money at all. "I was afraid," he murmured to his disappointed boss. "I knew you were demanding, so I buried my money in the ground to make sure I didn't lose it. See, sir, here it is." "You foolish servant!" the boss replied. "If you knew I was demanding, why didn't you put the money in a bank and at least earn interest? Take the money from this lazy employee and give it to the most productive one." The foolish servant didn't use what he had been given, and so he lost it.

Jesus, the narrator of this story, ends by saying, "To those who have, it will be given; but to those who do not have, even that which they have will be taken away" (Matthew 25:29). It's clear that the thrust of this story is that we must either use or lose our God-given talents. No middle ground exists. If we fail to make the effort, what we have will be taken from us and given to another.

Some would suggest this seems unfair. Let's face it: The first two servants had a significant advantage over the third. If the man with five talents lost one, he would have lost only 20 percent of his investment. Similarly, if the man with two talents lost one, it would mean he had lost 50 percent of his capital. But when you only have a single talent and you lose it, you're bankrupt; you've lost everything. So why penalize such a person for playing it safe? In fact, doesn't he deserve to be commended for not losing what he was given?

Perhaps the boss rebuked the servant for not trying. Not failure, but inaction, is sin. The successful servants weren't commended for not losing, but for being faithful. And one way this faithfulness manifested itself was in their willingness to make the attempt, to put forth the effort.

Those who have received God's comfort have something to share. When we look back to our times of disadvantage and remember God's mercies, we have something to share. Any Christian who has experienced God's solace during difficult times has a testimony, enabling him or her to use the pain of the past to bless others. You have an opportunity to lift a downcast gaze and a troubled heart by sharing with someone the ways God has comforted you (2 Corinthians 1:4). This is a talent we all can use for God's glory. Each of us has the capacity to be healers of the wounded.

Handle Competition Wisely

How well do you handle competition? Those who desire to use their talents well must learn to handle competition wisely. One of the first things to remember about competition is that God gives different abilities to different people. Some get five, others two, still others one. That's right; there is an inequality of gifts.

This knowledge should help us to focus our competitiveness on ourselves rather than on others. In other words, compete against yourself. The only person you should be trying to do better than is yourself.

John Wooden, the great UCLA basketball coach, emphasized this focus in his training. Eddie Powell, who played for and coached with John Wooden, remarked, "Coach Wooden was more upset if we won but didn't work up to our potential than if we lost playing at our best."[11] In fact, Wooden defined success as the "peace of mind which is a direct result of self-satisfaction in knowing you made the effort to become the best you are capable of becoming."[12]

Once you're wisely handling competition by competing against yourself, move to the next step by striving to serve. If you think of competition as an opportunity to serve, instead of seeking to be number one, you'll embrace a better perspective. This perspective is rooted in the knowledge that God expects us to serve (Galatians 5:13; 1 Peter 4:10). And what better way to serve than by using our God-given talents?

One of the things that helped me focus on serving was remembering that ownership is an illusion. The Bible reminds us that human beings come into this world with nothing and leave with the same amount (1 Timothy 6:7). What we think we own we'll eventually leave behind when we die. The fact is we're merely supervising that which God has loaned us, for what do we have that we have not been given (1 Corinthians 4:7)?

The correct perspective on competition also entails seizing opportunities to use our talents. Nehemiah is a great example of how to do this. This great leader had a prominent position in Persia, working directly for the king, when he heard that the walls of Jerusalem needed rebuilding (Nehemiah 1). Instead of waiting for someone else to take on this daunting task, he used the leverage of his high position to get the resources needed to accomplish it.

Are you handling competition by seizing opportunities to grow and develop your abilities so you can more effectively serve others? During my last two years of high school, which I spent at a boarding academy in rural Pottstown, Pennsylvania, I passionately desired to be a preacher. I was young and didn't have much opportunity to preach, but there were options. Throughout the day, I went into a wooded area where I could be alone. There I would practice my fledgling sermons with the trees as my congregation. By the time I finally began to study the science of preaching in college, those many hours spent preaching to the trees had provided me with a valuable head start in my effort to be the best preacher I could be. Use your talents well by seizing opportunities.

Take Judicious Risks

Using your talents to their fullest often involves taking judicious risks. I have already discussed the difference between judicious risk and foolish risk (see chapter 10). The former involves acting from past experience and with a backup plan in mind. David took a judicious risk when he went to fight Goliath (1 Samuel 17). He had much less fighting experience than his adversary, but God had given him success in previous battles. While tending his father's sheep, a lion and a bear attacked him on separate occasions, and God's Spirit enabled him to prevail over these predators. So much was at stake for his nation that it would have been easy to falter or back down, but God's past blessings provided David with the assurance that Jehovah wouldn't let him fail.

When I decided to become a navy chaplain, it was with a similar confidence in God—and despite the intense protest of several of my mentors. I chose not to follow their advice and entered the military ministry, keeping in mind that my initial contract was for three years. I knew that if my ministry experience was unrewarding, I could leave the chaplaincy and pursue a backup plan for my career. An investment of three years was a risk I was willing to take. As it turned out, I never had to use my backup plan. I discovered that I loved military ministry and remained in this arena for more than twenty-five years.

God blessed my willingness to take a risk, and I became a leader in military ministry. Some who had once advised me not to venture forward into a supposedly risky ministry congratulated me for how God was using my military work. They seemed to forget they had advised me to do nothing, to stay put, but my life was immeasurably enriched because I sailed into the uncharted waters of a new career.

Make Faithfulness Your Goal

Are you faithful? If you wish to use your talents for God's glory, make faithfulness your goal. Webster's Dictionary defines *faithful* as being loyal, trustworthy, conscientious, and thorough in the performance of duty. In short, your faithfulness is a measure of how much God can depend on you. If you're a parent, you know that some children are more trustworthy than others. One you can trust with the car keys and another you can't. One may be reliable three out of five times, or perhaps four out of six. In a similar way, some children of God are more dependable than others and can be entrusted by God with greater tasks. How dependable are you? In the matter of faithfulness, we are all on a level playing field. Regardless of what talents we may think we lack, God's standard of faithfulness is attainable by everyone. Each of us can be dependable.

Dependability involves character, for your character means more to God than your accomplishments. In other words, righteousness matters. When Luke recorded how God selected Zechariah and Elizabeth to be John the Baptist's parents, he mentioned that they were righteous people (Luke 1:6). Their character mattered to God and influenced His choice.

Jonathan Edwards, an eighteenth-century theologian, seemed to know this, for as a young man he wrote the following resolution: "Live in such a way that if God sought one person on earth for a special assignment, He would select me!" That's incredible faithfulness.

Those who possess such character and faithfulness are reliable even when no one is checking up on them. When I was a boy, someone once told me that character is who you are in the dark. I believe that. Your actions behind closed doors are far more important than what you do while the world looks on.

Adapt to Varied Soils

The second story referred to by the new senator, the parable of the farmer in Matthew 13, has a similar theme to the parable of the talents: *use it or lose it*. In this second story, a farmer plants seeds that strike four kinds of soil: impenetrable, superficial, preoccupied, and prepared. Birds carry off the seeds from the first soil, while the seeds sprout but quickly perish in the superficial soil. The third soil produces a promising harvest that is choked by thorns, while the prepared soil produces beautifully—"some a hundredfold, some sixty, some thirty" (Matthew 13:23, NKJV).

This story has many valuable lessons. First, it teaches us that failure need never be permanent. Those who use their talents well may discover that 75 percent of the seeds sown will miss good soil, but faithfulness in sowing is what's most important. Second, this story teaches the importance of perseverance. The farmer continued to plant his seeds, even when the harvest seemed delayed. If the farmer had ended his sowing in frustration, he may have never found good soil. Third, this story teaches that we not only reap what we sow, but often more than we have sown. Though the majority of the seeds missed prepared soil, those that found good ground produced wonderfully. Moreover, this unstoppable law of sowing and reaping is something God has promised will continue until the end of time (Genesis 8:22). When we faithfully use our talents, a harvest is certain.

Dealing with varied soil requires deepening our spiritual roots. We see this with the seeds that fell among thorns on the preoccupied soil. The Bible says that the thorns are the cares of this life, the deceitfulness of riches, and the concerns for material things that choke good seeds (Matthew 13:22). These difficulties destroy the seeds because they lack roots.

How important is it to develop spiritual roots? Jesus suggested it is critical when He talked about the houses that faced a storm (Matthew 7:24-27). One house collapsed, while the other stood firm. The one that survived symbolizes those who have deep roots and a firm foundation based upon hearing, understanding, and doing God's Word. Those who seek to use their talents for God will need the solid foundation that comes from hearing and heeding God's Word. This will prepare us for the varied soils we encounter in life.

You can't deepen your spiritual roots by seeking God only on weekends. Looking at the life of Christ, one can't help but be impressed by His vibrant devotional life. He maintained superb spiritual fitness. Luke 5:16 tells us that Jesus often withdrew to seek His Father in prayer at a solitary place, sometimes before daybreak (Mark 1:35). At times, He spent all night in prayer (Luke 6:12). His spiritual roots were deep and firm, enabling Him to "endure the cross, despising the shame for the joy that was set before Him" (Hebrews 12:2). We need to follow Christ's example and deepen our spiritual roots so that we can endure our trials, pursue joy, and use our pain to bless others.

As we prepare to deepen our roots, we should remember that in life all we can really do is plant and water seeds. The apostle Paul reminds us that, although people plant and water, only God can bring a harvest (1 Corinthians 3:6). When we use our talents well, we're planting seeds, and God has promised a harvest (Galatians 6:7-9). So we're admonished not to become weary in doing well, "for in due season we will reap if we don't faint" (Galatians 6:9).

Eighteenth-century British prime minister William Pitt planted and watered the seeds for the abolition of the slave trade in the heart of his friend William Wilberforce. The seeds germinated, and for twenty years Wilberforce spoke against the slave trade, until the British Parliament acted to outlaw it.

What seeds are you planting? My mother encouraged my brothers and sisters and me to memorize God's Word. As the years pass, I continue to be nurtured by those wonderful seeds. After teaching at the U.S. Senate Bible study one Thursday, I found myself reflecting on the Bible verses I had quoted. I realized that I had memorized most of them before entering ninth grade. What a wonderful harvest God has brought from my mother's faithful planting and watering. It has helped me deal with life's varied soils.

Don't Waste the Leftovers

The parables of the talents and of the farmer remind me of a third Gospel story—actually, an anecdote from a larger story: the moment when Jesus encouraged His disciples not to lose the leftover fragments from feeding the five thousand. After He miraculously multiplied the loaves and fish, which one little boy had brought for a meal, in order to satisfy an immense crowd, He said to His disciples, "Don't waste the leftovers" (John 6:12), and they filled twelve baskets with fragments. When I first read this part of the story, it puzzled me. If you have enough power to miraculously multiply food, why would you keep leftovers? Who wants day-old fish and bread anyway? With Jesus possessing such supernatural power, wouldn't there be plenty more where the first food came from? But Jesus wants us to waste none of our blessings, even the gifts of trials and trouble.

Paul and Silas didn't waste the leftovers of their pain; they used them for God's glory. Beaten and unfairly jailed, they sang praises to God around midnight until the other prisoners heard them and were transformed (Acts 16:25). This transformation was so significant that when an earthquake enabled the prisoners to escape, they stayed behind bars (Acts 16:28). What leftover blessings are you neglecting to gather and use for God's honor? You must use them or you will lose them.

Perhaps instead of neglecting leftover blessings you are wasting the leftovers of your time. Someone once asked the great jurist Oliver Wendell Holmes for a success tip. He responded, "Learn to use the fragments of your time." This is valuable advice. How many of our time fragments go unused? We spend time in the credit union lines or in traffic or waiting for a flight to take off or for a table in a restaurant. These are time fragments that we should be using instead of losing.

A few days ago, I ran into a high school friend, who gave me a useful piece of advice about the skillful use of time fragments. I had just finished speaking at a conference, and he was one of the interpreters, translating my talk into French, but he also did work in German. We had a delightful conversation, and I learned that he had gone to France, earned a PhD at the Sorbonne, and was not only multilingual but also an expert on Anicius Manlius Boethius, the sixth-century medieval philosopher.

"I wish I could speak several languages fluently," I said to him wistfully.

"You can," he assured me. "I simply found fifteen to twenty minutes each day to concentrate on learning a new language. By the end of the year, with this small time investment, I could converse easily in my new language." Isn't that amazing? Surprisingly, fragments of time used consistently can bring a bountiful harvest.

What about the leftovers of compassion? The people in the story of the feeding of the five thousand may have never been fed if Jesus hadn't spoken up. Christ possessed a compassion that His disciples lacked. He wouldn't let these people leave without feeding them. He said to His disciples, "Where can we find bread to feed these people?" (John 6:5). How many people continue to hurt because of our failure to use the leftovers of our compassion?

When we're watching television, we often come across a program about hungry children in third world countries. It's easy to become desensitized to such programs and reach for the remote control to change the channel. In many major cities, panhandlers beg for food and money every day. It's possible to see these people so often that we can pass by them unmoved. But we must be like Jesus and feel compassion for those in pain around us. This doesn't mean giving foolishly to professional beggars. It does mean continuing to feel their pain and continuing to look for creative ways to meet their needs. It means not forgetting that the lost and lonely in our world are our brothers and sisters, and that God will one day judge us for how we treat the "least of these."

Gather Fragments of Faith, Contentment, and Grace

Even with faith itself, we must use or lose. It took a little boy's faith to feed the multitude. No one would have taken his lunch from him; he had to give his permission, and he voluntarily gave it to Jesus. This boy possessed faith, an attribute without which we can't please God (Hebrews 11:6). Are you using the fragments of your faith?

Many years ago, I attended a fifty-member church in Annapolis, Maryland. The pastor asked me to conduct an evangelistic meeting, and I said yes. We began to discuss with the church elders where we should have the meeting. One of the elders startled us by saying, "Why not rent the Navy and Marine Corps stadium?" Now, on a good weekend, we might get thirty-five people attending our services, but this church officer wanted us to rent a stadium that could seat tens of thousands. Had he inhaled something? He had not. He simply had far more faith than we could imagine. Instead of renting the stadium, we held the meeting at a small local church, and God blessed our evangelistic outreach with ten baptisms—but I often wonder what the harvest would have been if we had stepped out in faith and rented the stadium. Who knows what God will accomplish for those who use faith's leftovers? He desires to do for us more than we can ask or imagine (Ephesians 3:20), but we must have faith to access such blessings.

What about your faith? Are you falling short of God's ideal will for your life by failing to let your reach exceed your grasp? What blessings have you failed to receive from God only because you didn't ask (James 4:2)? Why not maximize your possibilities by gathering the fragments of your faith?

Gather not only the fragments of your faith but also of your contentment. When Jesus fed the multitude, the Bible says they ate until they were satisfied (John 6:12). Jesus brings satisfaction

BARRY C. BLACK

and contentment, for He came so that we might live abundantly (John 10:10). This abundant living involves finding contentment and using its fragments to bless others.

How contented are you? Recently my wife and I stayed at a hotel we had not visited for some time. We noticed that in each of the three rooms of our suite the television had been upgraded to a flat screen. We enjoyed the big screen and the picture clarity. When I returned home, I was less enthusiastic about the viewing experience on my old television set. I was no longer content with what I had. "We need some new televisions," I intoned to my wife. "The ones we have are so old; flat screens would be so much better." I'd momentarily forgotten the wisdom of Ecclesiastes 4:6: "Better is a handful with contentment than two handfuls with vexation of spirit." I didn't need a new television as much as I suddenly thought I did.

I listened to a senator make a speech in the Chamber that showed me this man had learned contentment. He talked about excessive governmental spending before declaring, "My wife and I have lived in the same home since 1972. We've always lived on less money than we earned." He seemed satisfied not to go for that second handful.

In addition to those fragments of faith and contentment, we must use or lose the fragments of God's grace. When Paul battled the pain of his thorn in the flesh, God told him, "My grace is sufficient for you" (2 Corinthians 12:9, NIV). The five thousand were fed by the grace of Christ. Each of us has received this grace and should be willing to share it with others. God's Word reminds us: "Freely you have received, freely give" (Matthew 10:8, NIV). One of the reasons it's so important to comfort others with the comfort God has given us (2 Corinthians 1:4) is that it is a means of gathering and using fragments of grace.

A condemned thief received some of these grace fragments. Dying on a cross one Friday, he looked to the man in the middle. Watching the suffering man beside him transformed this thief, and he cried out for some grace fragments: "Lord, remember me when You come into Your kingdom" (Luke 23:42, NKJV).

How about you? Have you received God's grace? Jesus said, "What do you benefit if you gain the whole world but lose your own soul?" (Mark 8:36, NLT). Eternal life is worth any sacrifice, and it can be yours if you gather the fragments of God's grace. Then you will truly see blessing in your adversity.

AN ACTION PLAN TO HELP YOU USE IT (SO YOU DON'T LOSE IT)

> *Handle competition wisely.*

> *Take judicious risks.*

> *Make faithfulness your goal.*

> *Adapt to varied soils.*

> *Don't waste the leftovers.*

> *Gather fragments of faith, contentment, and grace.*

14

MASTER YOUR LIFE MAP

It was the best Christmas gift my son had ever given me: a Garmin global positioning system (GPS). This compact unit has a delightful female voice that helps me successfully navigate through dense traffic in the various cities where I have speaking engagements. Garmin has brought me joy, making me feel as if a companion is traveling with me. Even when I'm far from home, her soothing voice makes me feel connected to a higher source. You see, I have problems following even good directions, so my new traveling companion has dramatically simplified my life on the road.

At least that's how I felt until I arrived one day in Tennessee. I knew my hotel was only fifteen minutes from the airport, but nevertheless I hooked up my trusted navigational device before hitting the road. My usually reliable friend advised me to travel straight ahead for a hundred miles. "Something strange is happening here," I whispered to myself. I later learned that my GPS needed some vital maps that hadn't been downloaded. She was, therefore, clueless about where we should go. I stopped and asked for directions, verifying that I was only a few miles from my destination.

As we attempt to reach our eternal destination, we need a navigation aid, a life map. God has provided us with this vital aid in the Holy Bible, and we need to trust it for guidance. This wonderful book speaks about itself, declaring that it's "useful for teaching, rebuking, correcting and training in righteousness" (2 Timothy 3:16-17, NIV). Why? It's intended to prepare and equip us to do good works.

We can trust the Bible as our life map because it's useful for teaching. In other words, it shows us what's right. The ability to distinguish right from wrong is important to successful living. When God gave Solomon the opportunity to ask Him for anything (1 Kings 3), the young man asked for wisdom and the ability to know right from wrong. He earnestly desired to possess the ability to effectively lead his people through nuanced challenges, and his request pleased God. God's Word provides opportunities to improve our ethical IQ. It's good for teaching.

We can also trust the Bible as our life map because it provides rebuke, pointing out what's wrong. Sometimes we're not sure when something is wrong because we don't have a direct scriptural command to follow. For example, the Bible doesn't have a command against cigarettes or marijuana or blackjack. Without clear precepts and commands to point out what's wrong, we may have difficulty dealing with life's ethical gray areas.

Fortunately, our biblical life map provides not only commands, but also principles. Principles can be applied to many specific issues about which we may be in doubt. For example, even though the Bible doesn't mention cigarettes, 1 Corinthians 6:12 provides a principle we can apply: "All things are permissible, but not every-thing is beneficial. All things are permissible, but I will not be mastered by anything."

You can see how easy this becomes. We simply need to ask our-selves, "Are cigarettes beneficial?" That's an easy one. The Surgeon General warns on every package, "Cigarette smoking is dangerous to your health." If you accept that statement, smoking is certainly not beneficial. Not only that, but the addictive power of nicotine is well documented. Thank God for the scriptural precepts and principles that provide guidance for living.

A third reason we can trust the Bible as our life map is that it's good for correcting. In other words, it straightens us out by providing clear stepping-stones to right living, as opposed to just telling us what to do and what not to do. For example, the Bible says we should teach our children ethical principles, but then it goes on to show us how: "Memorize His laws and tell them to your children over and over again. Talk about them all the time, whether you're at home or walking along the road or going to bed at night, or getting up in the morning" (Deuteronomy 6:6-7).

The fourth benefit our Bible life map provides us is training in righteousness. This training is intended to help us finish what we've started. God is not interested primarily in a good start, but in a successful finish. Hebrews 12:2 calls Jesus the Author and Finisher of our faith. By following scriptural precepts and prin-ciples, we prepare ourselves to finish our life's race successfully. Those who benefit from these four characteristics will be equipped to do good works.

Receive Daily Spiritual Nourishment

How often do you study your life map? Matthew 6:11 teaches us to pray for our daily bread. This petition refers not only to physical food but also to spiritual nourishment. To receive proper spiritual nourishment, we need daily exposure to God's Word.

I have a friend who is a gifted musician. Her children have followed her example and have also excelled musically. One reason for their success is their mother's insistence on practice, practice, and more practice. I asked her, "How do you get your children to practice so consistently?"

She responded with a smile, "I simply tell them, 'Any day you eat, you practice.' It seems to work."

That's great advice for spiritual growth as well. Any day we eat physical food, we must also eat spiritual food. But how do we keep variety in eating? After all, if we had a bowl of the same cereal for breakfast every day, it would probably become tedious. We can keep variety in our spiritual nourishment by finding different ways to eat the marvelous food of God's Word. We can listen to it using CDs or portable MP3 players. We can also move beyond just reading to studying. Studying is when we delve deeply into a passage, highlighting and underlining key points and writing our thoughts in the margins.

When I'm asked to preach at the funeral of someone I didn't know, I ask to see his or her personal Bible. Believe it or not, I can actually get to know a person by reading what was written in his or her Bible. This enables me to deliver a eulogy with the feeling that I've come to know the deceased. Frequently people comment on how personal the eulogy seemed, not knowing that I was assisted by the diligent scriptural studies of the departed.

We can hear God's Word, and we can read it and study it. We can also memorize Scripture, hiding God's Word in our hearts (Psalm 119:11). Colossians 3:16 reminds us to let God's Word "dwell in you richly" (NIV). We do that when we memorize Scripture. We can then go beyond memorization to meditation, reflecting on what we know from the Word, turning over the precepts and principles in our minds. Psalm 1:1-2 says that blessed people meditate on God's Word day and night. By variously hearing, reading, studying, memorizing, and meditating on God's Word, we can create variety in our daily spiritual meals.

Find Spiritual Cleansing in God's Word

When we trust the Bible as our life map, we discover its cleansing power. God has chosen His revealed Word to purify the lives of His people and His church. John 17:17 states, "Sanctify them by Your truth. Your word is truth" (NKJV). We experience the phenomenon of sanctification through exposure to sacred literature. Ephesians 5:25-27 continues this emphasis: "Husbands, love your wives, just as Christ loved the church and gave himself up for her to make her holy, cleansing her by the washing with water through the word, and to present her to himself as a radiant church, without stain or wrinkle or any other blemish, but holy and blameless" (NIV).

Isn't that wonderful? God cleanses His church by the power of His Word. Perhaps this is one reason why most churches seem to have deficiencies; members are going through the cleansing process. Matthew 13:30 says that the wheat and tares must grow together until the harvest. In other words, don't expect a church filled with perfect people. Trust God's cleansing process.

A man once approached the great British preacher Charles Spurgeon and said, "Could you help me find the perfect church? Is your church the perfect church, Mr. Spurgeon?"

"No," Spurgeon responded. "My church is far from perfect. But when you find the perfect church, sir, please don't join it, because it would no longer be perfect."

The fact is that the church is not an art gallery of finished saints; it's a hospital where those who are hurt and bruised by life can find healing. One of God's primary ways of bringing about this healing is through the power of His Word.

Do you cherish the cleansing power of God's Word? Does the knowledge that sacred Scripture is a sanctifying force infuse you with confidence? If it does, be like the Bereans. They listened to Paul preach, but later they searched the Scriptures for themselves to check up on what the apostle had said (Acts 17:11).

Avoid the Pain of Shame

One of the great blessings of trusting God's Word as a life map is that it enables us to avoid the pain of shame. The psalmist declares, "Oh, that my ways were steadfast in obeying your decrees! Then I would not be put to shame when I consider all your commands" (Psalm 119:5-6, NIV).

Think of the biblical characters who faced the pain of shame. Noah was embarrassed by his naked drunkenness (Genesis 9), and Abraham lied and pretended his wife Sarah was his sister (Genesis 12). Moses had to flee from his home country after committing murder (Exodus 2), and David was guilty of the dual sins of adultery and murder (2 Samuel 11). The Bible doesn't airbrush its heroes and heroines, but provides candid portraits, warts and all.

In our own society, we have seen numerous examples of politicians and religious leaders who have been embarrassed by ethical missteps. We're all familiar with the usual television spectacle—the disgraced leader standing humbled by media scrutiny, with his stoic wife by his side, seeming so uncomfortable in the negative spotlight. How true is the biblical maxim, "The way of the transgressor is hard" (Proverbs 13:15, ASV).

How can you read the Bible in a way that will help you avoid the pain of shame? First, find a contemporary translation. Go to a Bible bookstore and read different translations until you find one that really appeals to you. Second, concentrate on what you're reading. If you were talking to an important person, you'd eliminate all distractions. Imagine trying to send text messages while talking to a senator or the president. Give God the courtesy of your undivided attention. Third, as you read, seek to discover what God is saying to you. Fourth, talk to God about what you're reading. In other words, pray the Scriptures. These four tactics will help you master your life map sufficiently to avoid the pain of shame.

Battle Temptation

Trusting your life map will provide you with a weapon to battle temptation and sin. This is an awesome benefit of Bible study: "I have hidden your word in my heart that I might not sin against you" (Psalm 119:11, NIV). Are you using this life map in a way that makes you armed and dangerous?

Jesus did. When He was tempted in the wilderness by Satan (Matthew 4), He used only one weapon in His defense: God's Word. He could have used logic or philosophy, but instead He repeatedly declared to His enemy, "It is written." If Jesus thought so much of God's Word that He used it as His sole weapon against the devil, shouldn't we do the same?

In Ephesians 6, the Bible describes the weapons in our spiritual arsenal. Each of these is defensive in nature, except one: "The sword of the Spirit, which is the word of God" (Ephesians 6:17, NIV). God's Word is a powerful weapon that will keep us armed and dangerous as we battle principalities and powers. Do you think of God's Word as a weapon? It can provide you with the offense you need when you're involved in spiritual warfare. You can send the devil running, as Jesus did, by responding to his overtures with a simple "It is written . . ."

For twenty years, King Saul pursued David, attempting to kill him. David was a fugitive, forced to be away from loved ones as he fled for his life. Twice he had opportunities to kill King Saul, but he refused to do so. His soldiers urged him to kill the king, but David responded, "I will not lift my hand against the Lord's anointed" (1 Samuel 24:10). David eventually defeated his enemy Saul by permitting God's Word to guide his conduct. Perhaps he was referring to this fact when he wrote, "Your commands make me wiser than my enemies, for they are ever with me" (Psalm 119:98, NIV).

Interestingly, David not only defeated his enemy, but he also loved him. He was obeying a principle that Jesus would later emphasize in the New Testament: love for those who spitefully use us (Matthew 5:44). How do we know David loved King Saul, his enemy? When Saul died, David mourned the monarch's death (2 Samuel 1). He was guided by his life map, God's Word, in his treatment of his predecessor.

Practice Restraint
As you're guided by this amazing life map, it will help you to develop an admirable restraint and to learn to err on the side of caution. Sometimes we don't have enough respect for the power of evil. Often our greatest protection against sin is a wholesome respect for its power, which will prompt us to exercise prudence and caution. The psalmist comments on this: "I have kept my feet from every evil path so that I might obey your word" (Psalm 119:101, NIV).

I like the notion of avoiding the path of evil. It suggests that appropriate caution entails not simply keeping away from sin's destination, but not even getting on the road that leads to transgression. This is what Joseph was doing when he not only resisted the wicked advances of Potiphar's wife, but refused even to be alone in a room with her (Genesis 39:10).

Do you trust your life map to the extent that it is keeping your feet from every evil path? That word *every* is important, for it strongly hints that partial obedience is disobedience. You must give God the benefit of your doubts by avoiding habits that will hinder your spiritual progress.

AN ACTION PLAN TO HELP YOU MASTER YOUR LIFE MAP

> *Receive daily spiritual nourishment.*

> *Find spiritual cleansing in God's Word.*

> *Avoid the pain of shame.*

> *Battle temptation.*

> *Practice restraint.*

15

FIND SATISFACTION

THE ROLLING STONES famously "can't get no satisfaction." But if multimillionaire rock stars find fulfillment elusive, how slender are the chances for us ordinary people? Perhaps Henry David Thoreau was right when he said, "The mass of men lead lives of quiet desperation." Must this be the destiny of the multitudes? Must we live life without joy and contentment?

Jesus came to bring contentment to the world. He said, "I came that they may have life and have it abundantly" (John 10:10, ESV). He made a greater impact on humanity than anyone else in all of history, and He intended for people to find satisfaction. In Matthew 11:28, He invites all who feel weary and heavy laden to find rest with Him. And in John 4, He leads a much-married woman at a Samaritan well from sadness to satisfaction. This amazing encounter provides wonderful principles for finding satisfaction in our own lives. Discovering contentment and satisfaction is a critical step in protecting our spiritual consecration.

What lessons can we learn about satisfaction from the woman at the well?

Reach Out to People Who Are Different

Sometimes we don't find satisfaction because we neglect to reach out to people who are different. Perhaps we associate only with those from our economic, social, or racial backgrounds. That's a mistake that Jesus didn't make. On one of His journeys, He went by way of Samaria—something the Jews of His day would have avoided at all costs. But Jesus ventured off the beaten track to bring eternal satisfaction to a Samaritan woman. Later, He revealed His personal satisfaction when He told His disciples, "I have meat to eat of which you are unaware" (John 4:32). He experienced something that satisfied His physical hunger, even as the woman received something that satisfied her soul.

When we reach out to those who are different, particularly the less fortunate, we often develop a greater appreciation for what we possess. Someone said, "I felt sorry for myself because I had no shoes, until I met a man who had no feet." Those who desire to learn contentment and find satisfaction should reach out to others.

Blessing others can have positive eternal consequences. One U.S. senator has led many African heads of state to Jesus Christ. His outreach to these key foreign leaders has paid eternal dividends.

Expect God to Take the Initiative

The second lesson we can learn from John 4 is to expect God to take the initiative. Jesus says in another place, "No one comes to God except the Father draws him or her" (John 6:44). This amazing statement reminds us that God is our pursuer. How foolish we are to worry about what will happen to our loved ones when God is more interested in their well-being than we are. He has thousands of ways to make His purposes clear to humanity, for even the heavens declare His glory (Psalm 19:1).

Jesus pointed out to His disciples that their relationship with Him came from what He initiated: "Ye have not chosen me," He said, "but I have chosen you" (John 15:16, KJV). In a sense, this can be said for the selection of every disciple. Jesus took the initiative with the woman at the well, and He does the same with us. It is this same initiative that inspired Francis Thompson to write the poem "The Hound of Heaven," which pictures God's relentless pursuit of humanity as a tracking hound, following us wherever we go. And God's initiative can lead us to the satisfaction of a desired destination (Jeremiah 29:11). As you long for satisfaction, know that God is constructively working behind the scenes of your life.

Overcome Barriers to Unity

The third lesson on the road to satisfaction is this: Overcome barriers to unity. Psalm 133:1 states, "How good and pleasant it is for brothers and sisters to dwell together in unity." Lack of unity is the root of much discontentment. Those who desire to find satisfaction would do well to remove impediments to unity.

Abraham removed these impediments in his family (Genesis 13:8). When Abraham's herdsmen couldn't get along with his nephew Lot's workers, Abraham proposed a unifying solution. Lot should have acted first, but he didn't. After all, Lot owed his uncle a great deal. It was Abraham whom God had chosen to be the father of a great nation, and it was Abraham whom God had inspired to leave Ur and head for Canaan. Lot had simply followed along, and he became wealthy primarily because of his association with Abraham. His gratitude to his uncle should have motivated him to take the initiative in defusing the dispute among their herdsmen. Instead, Abraham, the older and wealthier man, removed the barriers to unity.

Jesus did something similar with the Samaritan woman at the well. Her belief that Jesus was the Messiah became a catalyst for removing the barrier of race and eventually prompting many of the people of her town to accept Him as their Savior, in spite of their differences in race and history. When she played the race card, Jesus refused to be drawn in by her polemic. She had responded to His request for water with these words: "You are a Jew and I am a Samaritan woman. How can you ask me for a drink?" (John 4:9, NIV). For the Jews did not associate with Samaritans. Jesus met this challenge by inviting the woman to sample living water that would permanently quench her thirst. By leading the woman to a satisfaction she had sought but not found, Jesus overcame a barrier to unity.

Expect Satisfaction

The story's fourth lesson is to *expect* satisfaction. When Jesus talked to the woman about satisfying, living water, He awakened in her an expectation. He said to her, "If you knew the gift of God and who it is that asks you for a drink, you would have asked him and he would have given you living water" (John 4:10, NIV). We miss satisfaction by failing to expect it and by discontinuing our search for living water. Setting the bar too low, we live beneath our spiritual privilege.

We also live beneath our privilege by failing to ask God for satisfaction. James 4:2 warns about failing to make a request: "Ye have not, because ye ask not" (KJV). And our failure to ask is a result of diminished expectations. As the lyrics of one blues song put it, "I've been down so long that up ain't on my mind."

Pursuers of God should expect satisfaction. In his *Confessions*,

Saint Augustine declares to God, "You have made us for yourself, and our heart is restless until it rests in you."[13] In short, Augustine declares that only God can fill the God-shaped void in our hearts. Though we may try to fill the void with food, drugs, human relationships, money, and possessions, none of these substitutes will fill it. None will bring us deep and abiding satisfaction. Only God can fill us with satisfaction, and we should expect that He will.

Don't Underestimate God

Lesson five is don't underestimate God. The woman at the well did by seeking to place limits on what Jesus could do. "Sir," she said, "you have nothing to draw with and the well is deep. Where can you get this living water?" (John 4:11, NIV). Have you missed satisfaction because you've placed limits on God?

Israel's enemies once made such a mistake. They were fighting God's people and experienced defeat in mountainous terrain. They concluded, "We are losing because Israel's God is a mountain deity. Let's get them in the valley and we will win." God told His people, "Because your enemies have underestimated Me, I'll defeat them in the valley also" (1 Kings 20:28).

Those who find satisfaction know that God is not just in charge of mountaintop experiences. In fact, He is often closest to us in life's valleys, using our pain to bless others. He brings victories in the valleys of disappointment, grief, sickness, and pain. God's work in life's valleys led Job to say, "He knows the way that I take; when He has tested me, I shall come forth as gold" (Job 23:10, NKJV).

Begin at Home

Lesson six: Begin at home. Who has said on his or her deathbed, "I wish I'd spent more time at the office?" Yet we often live as if our work is more important than our families. To the woman at the well, Jesus said, "Go, call your husband and come back" (John 4:16, NIV). I'm not certain why Jesus asked this Samaritan woman to go get her husband. Perhaps He wanted her to face and admit the pain of five failed marriages and the dead-end street of her current living arrangement. Whatever Jesus' intentions may have been, His efforts to transform this woman began with raising the issue of her home life.

On another occasion, when Jesus exorcised demons from a man, the man immediately requested to go with Jesus (Luke 8:26-39). Can you understand why? He didn't want to stay in a place where his reputation had been besmirched by his insanity. Jesus refused his request. Instead, He told the man to go home and let his family and neighbors know about the transformation he had undergone through contact with the divine Healer.

In Acts 1:8, Jesus tells His disciples about the Holy Spirit's coming: "You will be witnesses unto me, first in Jerusalem, then Judea and Samaria, then to the uttermost parts of the world." Telling Jewish men to share the Good News first in Jerusalem meant sharing first with their own family members, relatives, and acquaintances. Those who find satisfaction must not neglect to share it with those closest to them.

Let It Show

One of the final themes of Jesus' conversation with the woman at the well is worship. He said to her, "God is spirit, and his worshipers must worship in spirit and in truth" (John 4:24, NIV). Our worship may reflect the orthodoxy of truth and yet lack spiritual passion.

David worshiped passionately in the Spirit. In 2 Samuel 6:14, he dances before the Lord, unashamed to give God unbridled praise, even when criticized. Some of my friends eschew "over the top" worship. "Barry," they say, "I'm more contemplative and cerebral in my worship. It's just my disposition." Yet when these same friends go to the secular sanctuary of a football stadium, their meditative demeanor disappears, and they exhibit an enthusiasm that seems uncharacteristic. How much more should they be enthusiastic about coming before the Lord in an attitude of worship? God expects us to "make a joyful noise" (Psalm 100:1, KJV). So worship in Spirit and in truth. If you're happy in Jesus, let it show on your face.

The Rolling Stones had it wrong; you *can* find satisfaction—but only in God, the one true source.

AN ACTION PLAN TO HELP YOU FIND SATISFACTION

> *Reach out to people who are different.*

> *Expect God to take the initiative.*

> *Overcome barriers to unity.*

> *Expect satisfaction.*

> *Don't underestimate God.*

> *Begin at home.*

> *Let it show.*

16

MASTER THE SPIRITUAL
DISCIPLINES

A FEW OFFICE WORKERS from Chicago grew tired of the vocational rat race and decided to become farmers. Leaving the high-rise behind, they purchased some acreage downstate and declared, "Now we're farmers." And all seemed right with the world. Each day, they went out and looked at their fields and felt proud of their new vocation. But they didn't plow or plant. When October rolled around and the neighboring farmers began to bring in the harvest, all the folks from Chicago had was forty acres of goldenrod and wildflowers.

"Where's the corn?" they asked. "What went wrong?"

What went wrong was that these worn-down white-collar workers from Chicago made the mistake of expecting a harvest without disciplined work.

In the same way, many people expect spiritual progress to be effortless. When they accept Jesus as Lord, they assume their lives will magically produce a harvest without spiritual plowing, planting, and watering (1 Corinthians 3:6). But spiritual growth requires work and a mastery of the spiritual disciplines.

How well are you doing with the spiritual disciplines? Can you see how your feelings of love for God have grown since you became a Christian? As time passes, you should love God in a more profound and nuanced way.

Immediately following my wedding, I thought I loved my bride more than life itself. Now, after thirty-six years of matrimony, as I consider how much deeper and solid my love is for my wife, I smile to think of the immaturity of my early affection for her. Similarly, as we grow in grace and in our knowledge of God (2 Peter 3:18), we should love Him more deeply.

Growth in love comes as we develop our spiritual fitness. In the same way we develop physical fitness through exercise and discipline, we must also work to acquire spiritual fitness. It is important to master the calisthenics needed for spiritual well-being, the spiritual push-ups, pull-ups, and sit-ups, as well as what we might call resistance training and cardio. A significant part of this spiritual workout involves mastering the spiritual disciplines.

Many Christians profess to want to live like Jesus. The desire is so great that some people try to guess what Jesus would do in various situations. Living like Jesus involves more than doing what He commanded, such as "love your enemies," or "turn the other cheek," or "pray for those who persecute you." Living like Jesus means doing what Jesus did. His life was characterized by a mastery of spiritual disciplines such as watching, prayer, study, meditation, silence, service, fasting, solitude, and worship. When you incorporate these and other spiritual disciplines into your life, then you are truly living like Jesus.

What is a spiritual discipline? For Christians, it's an activity undertaken to bring us into more effective cooperation with Christ and His Kingdom. Anything that accomplishes this goal makes a contribution to spiritual discipline.

Why are spiritual disciplines important? First, because Jesus left us an example of spiritual mastery that we should seek to know and emulate. The Bible says we should walk as Jesus walked (1 Peter 2:21; 1 John 2:6), following in His footsteps. How can Christians not learn how to pray, for example, when Jesus spent so much time in prayer (Luke 5:16)? Why do some refuse to fast when it's clear He expected His followers to do so (Matthew 6:16-18)? If the purest person who walked on our planet depended on prayer and fasting, who are we to neglect these disciplines?

Second, we should master the spiritual disciplines because they help us live abundantly (John 10:10). Why settle for less than abundant living when it is clearly Jesus' desire for His followers?

Third, we should master the spiritual disciplines because they lead to spiritual success and fitness. In Mark 9, Jesus' disciples make an unsuccessful attempt to cast a demon from a boy. After this failure, when they are alone with Jesus, they ask Him, "Why couldn't we cast out this demon?"

Jesus responds, "This kind comes out only by prayer and fasting" (Mark 9:29). Jesus made it clear to His disciples, and to us, that some spiritual battles require more than faith; they require a greater mastery of the spiritual disciplines. In 1 Timothy 4:7-8, Paul speaks of how this mastery leads to spiritual fitness: "Take time and trouble to keep spiritually fit. Bodily fitness has limited value, but spiritual fitness has unlimited value." Why is this so? Because bodily exercise has value only for this life. In eternity, we'll have new bodies, so spiritual fitness, which prepares us for the afterlife, is of greater value.

Develop Your Desire to Know God

How do we prepare to know God better? The first step is to develop a desire. You should strive to be like Moses, who sought a greater intimacy with God (Exodus 33:7-23), and strive to be more like David, who wrote, "As the deer pants for streams of water, so my soul pants for you, O God. My soul thirsts for God, for the living God. When can I go and meet with God?" (Psalm 42:1-2, NIV). Without a strong desire to know God, you will probably live beneath your spiritual privilege and hinder yourself from developing the power you need to gain significant spiritual success.

Let me relate a story that demonstrates the importance of knowledge. It takes place during the Great Depression. At that time, a sheep rancher in Texas was struggling to pay his bills. He had so little money that it seemed his only option was to file for bankruptcy. One day he was approached by a seismographic crew, who requested permission to drill on his land to see if they could find oil. He gave them permission, and it wasn't long before they discovered rich oil reserves beneath his land, which he sold to the oil company for an immense profit. This man, Mr. Yates, gained ownership of that rich oil reservoir when he purchased the land. But until he knew the oil existed, he lived dreadfully beneath his blessings. Similarly, getting to know God can lead us to treasures that bring abundant living. Perhaps this is what the apostle Paul sought when he said, "I want to know Christ and the power of His resurrection and the fellowship of His suffering, being conformed to Him in His death" (Philippians 3:10).

Where does the desire to know God better rank on your priority list? When you examine how you spend your time, what priority do you give to spiritual things? Those who want to master the spiritual disciplines must invest the time to develop a deeper knowledge of God.

Build on the Foundation of God's Word

Mastering the spiritual disciplines requires a firm foundation. The psalmist reveals that the best foundation we can have is God's Word. He writes, "I wait for the LORD, my soul waits, and in his word I put my hope" (Psalm 130:5, NIV). Like the psalmist, we should rest our hopes on God's Word. King Zedekiah learned this lesson the hard way (Jeremiah 37). Zedekiah made an unwise alliance with Egypt in an effort to protect his nation from defeat while at war with Babylon. He did this in spite of being warned by the prophet Jeremiah that Babylon would defeat Israel. The king ignored this word from God and had the prophet thrown in prison as a traitor. Zedekiah, however, knew that God's word would prevail, so he went secretly to Jeremiah with the question, "Is there any word from the LORD?" (Jeremiah 37:17, KJV). The prophet repeated the unpleasant warning, for God hadn't changed His mind, and Jeremiah's prediction came true.

Some years ago, I worked in an evangelistic meeting in Memphis. The key laborers in this meeting were called Bible Workers, and they visited with those who attended the meeting, explaining God's Word to those who were interested. The evangelist, following biblical principles (Luke 10), sent the Bible Workers out two by two, six teams in all. This seemed to me an inefficient way to use twelve people; however, the meeting's success showed me the wisdom of placing hope in God's Word. The number of baptisms that day set a Memphis record.

What is the foundation of your hope? What moral compass do you use to navigate life's treacherous shoals? Have you found a lamp for your feet and a light for your path (Psalm 119:105)? I strongly urge you to rest your hope in God's Word, for which there is no substitute.

Learn to Hate Evil

Is *hate* a four-letter word you try to avoid? It often seems difficult to find something constructive to say about such a seemingly ugly word. For Christians, however, there is an appropriate hatred, and that is the hatred of sin. Solomon puts it this way: "To fear the LORD is to hate evil; I hate pride and arrogance, evil behavior and perverse speech" (Proverbs 8:13, NIV).

How are you doing when it comes to hating sin? I must confess that I'm not all the way there yet. I dislike some sin, but feel drawn to other transgressions. This probably indicates a need for greater spiritual fitness, since hating sin comes from learning to see it as God does, in all of its repulsiveness.

It's easy to sanitize sin, to use euphemisms to describe evil. We speak about embezzlement instead of stealing, or an affair instead of adultery. We call pornography "adult entertainment" and refer to abortions as a matter of choice. The tendency toward euphemisms often mitigates the truly ugly nature of sin, making it more difficult to hate. Fortunately, Joseph's hatred of sin was sufficiently strong to resist the adulterous overtures of Potiphar's wife with these words: "How then can I do this great wickedness, and sin against God?" (Genesis 39:9, NKJV).

If you want to be like Joseph, ask yourself this question: "Am I a sheep or a pig?" What does that mean? Well, you can put sheep and pigs in mud and they react quite differently. The pig is in its element, but the sheep is unhappy. The closer you come to Jesus, the less pleased you'll be with wallowing in the mud of sin. You'll long to be cleansed by His righteousness—as quickly as possible.

Where are you on the continuum of hating sin? Are you moving closer to seeing transgression in all of its ugliness, even as God views it? Have many of the wicked things that once fascinated you lost their magnetic pull? As you work to master the spiritual disciplines, sin will become far less attractive.

Focus on Things Above

Master the spiritual disciplines by adopting an upward gaze. The apostle Paul offers some helpful counsel: "Set your minds on things above, not on earthly things" (Colossians 3:2, NIV). When we do this, it enables us to see life's challenges in their proper perspective. Paul endured more hardships than most Christians ever will. He was involved in at least three shipwrecks, stoned and left for dead, and scourged by the Romans in the same way Jesus was (2 Corinthians 11:25). Nonetheless, he viewed these painful encounters as "light afflictions which are only for a moment" (2 Corinthians 4:17). They mattered little in comparison to his heavenly reward.

No doubt Paul learned the power of the upward gaze from Jesus. When soldiers came to arrest Jesus, Peter tried to defend Him by cutting off the ear of the high priest's servant (John 18:10). Jesus said to His disciple, "Put away your sword, for don't you know that right now I could pray to My Father, and He would send twelve legions of angels to defend Me?" (Matthew 26:52-53). Though Jesus was faced with the horrific reality of His impending death, He kept His gaze fixed on heavenly things.

Where is your focus? How often during the week do you think about heaven? How often during your day do you think about spiritual things? When you miss your Bible study time, do you feel the deficit? Does it make you hungry enough to make up for it, even if it means missing out on an earthly desire or priority? If you want to master the spiritual disciplines, set your focus on things above.

Cultivate Love for Others

Would you like a CliffsNotes version of the Bible to help you master the spiritual disciplines? Here it is: "For all the law is fulfilled in one word, even in this: 'You shall love your neighbor as yourself'" (Galatians 5:14, NKJV). The law, in this instance, refers to God's revealed will. So we have a condensed version of all of Scripture in this command.

It's so important to love our neighbors that the Bible tells us we can't love God without loving one another. Listen to what it says: "If anyone says, 'I love God,' yet hates his brother, he is a liar. For anyone who does not love his brother, whom he has seen, cannot love God, whom he has not seen" (1 John 4:20, NIV). Those are harsh words, but they express the importance of having love for our fellow human beings.

This type of love goes beyond rhetoric, as the parable of the Good Samaritan indicates (Luke 10). In this well-known story, a wounded man is ignored by a priest and a Levite, but is cared for by a foreigner, a man of a despised race. This Samaritan binds the wounds of the wounded man and pays for his rehabilitation. This benefactor risks his personal safety in order to meet the needs of someone bleeding on the roadside. This is the pragmatic love we must develop if we're expecting to master the spiritual disciplines. Perhaps this is why the Bible says that love fulfills the law (Romans 13:10).

Practice Forgiveness

We're probably not ready to master the spiritual disciplines until we've cultivated our ability to practice forgiveness. In fact, our opportunity to receive divine forgiveness is linked to our willingness to forgive others, as is indicated in the Lord's Prayer: "Forgive us our debts, as we forgive our debtors" (Matthew 6:12, NKJV).

The first words Jesus uttered from the cross took the form of a prayer of forgiveness for His enemies: "Father, forgive them; for they know not what they do" (Luke 23:34, KJV).

When Jesus taught His disciples about forgiveness, Peter asked Him, "How many times should I forgive someone? Seven?" Jesus answered, "No, seventy times seven" (Matthew 18:21-22). In other words, continue to forgive until it becomes a habit.

I had problems forgiving my alcoholic father, and I stayed angry with him until he died. It was only after his death that I began to deal with my unloving feelings, and by God's grace, developed my capacity to forgive. In retrospect, I've wondered why I had such a difficult time forgiving him, particularly in light of how much God has forgiven me. Jesus summed up the proper behavior this way: "Do not judge, and you will not be judged. Do not condemn, and you will not be condemned. Forgive, and you will be forgiven" (Luke 6:37, NIV).

How are you doing in the area of forgiveness? Does your emotional baggage keep you from maximizing your spiritual possibilities? Forgive and you'll be forgiven, and then you will be better prepared to master the spiritual disciplines.

Obey God Fully

Be prepared to give God your all as you seek to master the spiritual disciplines. "If you fully obey the LORD your God and carefully follow all his commands I give you today, the LORD your God will set you high above all the nations on earth. All these blessings will come upon you and accompany you if you obey the LORD your God" (Deuteronomy 28:1-2, NIV). That's a serious mandate.

Sometimes we miss out on blessings because of only partial obedience. We're like Naaman, the Aramean army commander who had enough faith to visit the prophet Elisha for healing, but

THE BLESSING OF ADVERSITY

was reluctant to dip seven times in the Jordan River as the prophet advised (2 Kings 5). At first Naaman displayed only partial obedience, though at the urging of his servant, he eventually complied fully and was healed.

While I served in the Navy Chaplain Corps, I learned the military's core values. One of them is "Choose the harder right." That's great advice. If you're prepared to give your full measure of ethical devotion, why not choose the harder right, erring on the side of moral caution? That is great preparation for mastering the spiritual disciplines.

Are you giving God your all, or are you settling for partial obedience? Are you making a full commitment in your giving, in your marriage, parenting, and work? Choose the harder right and give God your all. The intensity of our devotion does matter, which is why we're told to love God with all our heart, soul, mind, and strength (Luke 10:27).

Serve Those in Need

One of my favorite television programs is a British comedy called *Are You Being Served?* The program is about zany happenings in a British department store, but the title reminds us of a question that Christians should frequently reflect upon: "Am I living a servant's life?"

God expects us to live as servants. Paul writes, "Be devoted to one another in brotherly love. Honor one another above yourselves. Never be lacking in zeal, but keep your spiritual fervor, serving the Lord. . . . Share with God's people who are in need. Practice hospitality" (Romans 12:10-13, NIV). Now, that's a tall order, isn't it? But honoring and serving one another constitutes great preparation for mastering the spiritual disciplines.

As we serve, let's remember that sometimes the greatest labor we can perform is to sit at Jesus' feet (Luke 10:40-42). Let's also remember that we're serving Christ, even when we do something as simple as give a cup of water in His name to someone in need (Mark 9:41).

Once, while watching players warm up before an NBA play-off game, I saw the great athlete LeBron James. He was earnestly practicing and preparing for the game just like his teammates. An announcer, having observed James's skill many times in the past, commented half seriously, "Why does he need to practice?" I found myself thinking, *Perhaps there's a connection between his practice and his greatness.*

What about you? Are you willing to prepare to practice the spiritual disciplines, or will you be like the Chicago farmers who expected to reap without sowing? Get ready to master the spiritual disciplines.

AN ACTION PLAN TO HELP YOU MASTER THE SPIRITUAL DISCIPLINES

> *Develop your desire to know God.*

> *Build on the foundation of God's Word.*

> *Learn to hate evil.*

> *Focus on things above.*

> *Cultivate love for others.*

> *Practice forgiveness.*

> *Obey God fully.*

> *Serve those in need.*

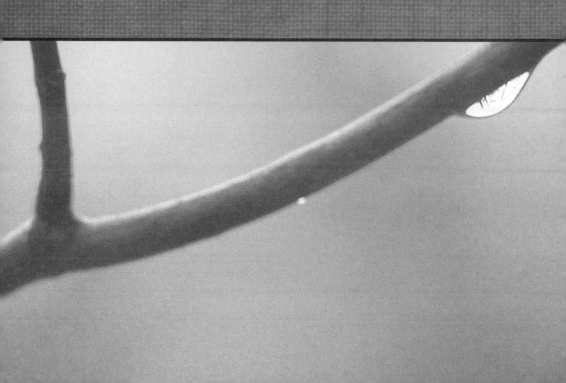

PART II:
Avoiding the Sources of Trouble

17

TAME YOUR TEMPTATIONS

Oscar Wilde, the infamous nineteenth-century Irish poet and libertine, reportedly said, "I can resist anything but temptation." Many of us feel the same way. Our promises and resolutions are like ropes of sand to which we can't cling. We long for insights that will enable us to tame temptation in our lives.

To prepare to find blessings in our trouble, it's essential that we tame temptation. God expects it. James 4:7 challenges us to "resist the devil, and he will flee from you" (NIV), and Ephesians 6:11 says, "Put on the whole armor of God that you may withstand Satan's wiles." So how can we tame temptation?

Know Your Enemy's Capabilities

I used to play chess, and I tended to lose more games than I won—until I shifted my focus. Finally I realized that instead of pursuing my own strategy independent of my opponent's actions, I should concentrate on countering my opponent's favorite strategies and tactics. With this new approach, I began winning more games than I lost.

Satan uses specific strategies against us. How well do you know them? Recognizing "the wiles of the devil" is a critical step in learning how to tame our temptations. Speaking of Satan, the apostle Paul said, "We are not ignorant of his devices" (2 Corinthians 2:11, NKJV).

What are his devices? First, he wants us to doubt God's Word. He used this strategy on Eve in the Garden (Genesis 3). Second, he wants us to feel capable of conquering sin through our own efforts, like Samson with Delilah (Judges 16). One of his favorite tactics is to attack us when we're vulnerable. After Jesus had fasted forty days and was weak with hunger, the devil came to tempt Him (Matthew 4:1-4). What are his favorite temptation weapons? First John 2:15-16 tells us that our enemy has a limited, but effective, repertoire: the lust of the flesh, the lust of the eyes, and the pride of life. Nearly every temptation includes one or more of these seductive overtures.

Consider Sin's Long-Term Consequences

Can you think of a time when you had to resist a temptation and regretted not succumbing? I have yet to meet a person who feels this way. In retrospect, we usually rejoice at our seemingly small victories over evil, for time often reveals sin's terrible long-term consequences. Even when Joseph was in prison, he never expressed regret at resisting the seductive banter of Potiphar's wife (Genesis 40). He considered sin's long-term consequences and asked, "How then can I do this great wickedness, and sin against God?" (Genesis 39:9, NKJV).

Who would embark on a journey that had a high probability of leading to death? Yet thousands regularly engage in sins that

---

promise destructive consequences. The Bible states, "The wages of sin is death" (Romans 6:23). Knowing this, no one should sin without considering its endgame—destruction.

Refuse to Rationalize

Too often we rationalize sin by finding socially acceptable reasons for our ethical misconduct. Instead of practicing integrity, we look for loopholes that will keep us from duty's tasks. Often we see ourselves as the exception to the rule. *Surely someone as important as I am deserves greater liberty than the less gifted and talented.* But God says, "Not so fast." Paul teaches that we should be guided by our conscience: "Whatsoever is not of faith is sin" (Romans 14:23, KJV). In other words, when we deviate from exercising faith in doing what we feel is right, we sin. We are to follow the light as God gives us the ability to see it, even when our theology may not be 100 percent correct. When we follow our faith and heart, theological correctness becomes secondary; for, on matters of doctrine, we all "see through a glass, darkly" (1 Corinthians 13:12, KJV). This is not to suggest that God has no absolutes, for the requirements of His laws are nonnegotiable. It does mean, however, that life can present us with gray areas—right vs. right conundrums that require us to hear the whispers of our conscience and proceed by faith to do what our hearts believe is best.

Run When Necessary

Paul advised his protégé Timothy, "Flee youthful lust and pursue righteousness, faith, love, and peace" (2 Timothy 2:22). To rid ourselves of temptation, sometimes it's necessary to run. Yes, sometimes it's appropriate to discuss the matter, but often it's better to flee. The Bible records that Potiphar's wife "caught [Joseph] by his cloak and said, 'Come to bed with me!' But he left his cloak in her hand and ran out of the house" (Genesis 39:12, NIV).

Often we neglect to follow Joseph's example of erring on the side of caution because we're too confident in our ability to stand toe-to-toe with temptation and win. The Bible warns against this mistake: "Let those who think they stand take heed lest they fall" (1 Corinthians 10:12). From this verse, we can infer that one of our greatest protections against sin is healthy fear and humility. Tame temptation by being willing to flee.

Be Willing to Experience Embarrassment

Will you do what is right even when it means facing embarrassment? King Herod wouldn't. He compromised his integrity to avoid embarrassment. At a birthday party for himself (Matthew 14), Herod desired Herodias's daughter to dance seductively for him and his guests. In the company of peers, he promised her up to half his kingdom if she would do his bidding, and she agreed. After the dance, Herod asked her, "What do you desire?" After consulting with her mother, she replied, "The head of John the Baptist on a platter."

Herod was mortified, but he had John executed rather than suffer embarrassment in front of his guests. If he had reneged on his offer, he would have lost face. Instead, he gave in to an expediency that snuffed out the life of one of the world's greatest prophets. We should be willing to experience embarrassment if it saves us from giving in to temptation.

Use the Power of Prayer

One of the most severe tests any human has ever undergone took place in the garden of Gethsemane. It was there that Jesus battled with cosmic forces, wielding one primary weapon: *prayer*

(Mark 14:32). He enlisted His disciples' aid, but they slept instead of interceding. So, left alone, Jesus gathered His strength for Calvary by harnessing the power of prayer.

This is not surprising. He had taught that prayer is the antidote for despair. He even told them a parable to show "they should always pray and not lose heart" (Luke 18:1). When life's problems overwhelm you, remember to tame temptation with prayer.

That is how Jesus tamed the temptation of Calvary. It is worth repeating that His first words from the cross were a prayer: "Father, forgive them; for they know not what they do" (Luke 23:34, KJV). Later He quoted Psalm 22:1: "My God, my God, why have you forsaken me?" (NIV). He was not making a cry of desolation, but praying the Scriptures. Prayer is a choice weapon for conquering temptation.

Find Accountability Partners

Jesus had friends with Him as He prayed in Gethsemane. Peter, James, and John were His accountability partners, people with whom He could be transparent and from whom He could receive encouragement. They had been with Jesus on many other important occasions, accompanying Him when He raised Jairus's daughter and on the mountain when He was transfigured.

Just like Jesus, we need to cultivate such friendships. There is power with a team. Perhaps this is one of the reasons Jesus sent His disciples out in groups of two (Luke 10). Two can almost always accomplish much more than one. As it says in Ecclesiastes, "Two people are better off than one, for they can help each other succeed. If one person falls, the other can reach out and help. But someone who falls alone is in real trouble. . . . A person standing alone can be attacked and defeated, but two can stand back-to-back and conquer" (4:9-10, 12, NLT). The combination has more power than the sum of its individual parts. Having partners who support us during the tough times can make the difference between victory and defeat.

Focus on God's Purposes

In Gethsemane, Jesus tamed temptation. He prayed, "Abba, Father, everything is possible for you. Take this cup from me. Yet not what I will, but what you will" (Mark 14:36, NIV). Focusing on God's will was the primary reason for His victory.

When we desire to do God's will and can see the unfolding of His purposes as we battle evil, it helps us prevail. Paul had an epiphany regarding his incarceration: "What is happening to me is for the furtherance of the gospel" (Philippians 1:12). In his unfair imprisonment, he saw an opportunity for God to triumph. These thoughts kept him from pessimism and despair and enabled him to tame temptation.

All things considered, I respectfully disagree with Oscar Wilde. By God's grace, I *can* resist anything, including temptation, for "I can do everything through Christ, who gives me strength" (Philippians 4:13, NLT).

AN ACTION PLAN TO HELP YOU TAME YOUR TEMPTATIONS

> *Know your enemy's capabilities.*

> *Consider sin's long-term consequences.*

> *Refuse to rationalize.*

> *Run when necessary.*

> *Be willing to experience embarrassment.*

> *Use the power of prayer.*
> *Find accountability partners.*
> *Focus on God's purposes.*

18

WIN OVER WORRY

IT'S DIFFICULT TO REMEMBER when the idea first entered my mind, but once it did, I was haunted by it: *You will not live longer than your father.* My father died at fifty-four, and the thought that my life wouldn't pass that fragile boundary frightened me.

With the passing of each birthday, the dreaded age approached, and when I finally reached it, I waited to exhale. Then I calculated how many months my father had lived beyond his fifty-fourth birthday, still thinking my life would end prematurely. Few people have experienced the joy I felt when my fifty-fifth birthday arrived.

In retrospect, it seems foolish for me to have worried about something so irrational. I had no evidence for my fear. What I did have was a superstitious anxiety that stole my peace. I spent years worrying about something that never happened.

Thousands battle with worry. We worry about health, retirement, our children and grandchildren, our leaders and nation, and eternity. We worry about the past, present, and future. Worry

THE BLESSING OF ADVERSITY

keeps us from achieving our maximum potential, paralyzing us with a stultifying fear.

Jesus came to set us free from worry. He addressed this issue in His Sermon on the Mount. In Matthew 6:25, He says, "Don't worry about your life." Afterward, He provided a blueprint for winning over worry.

Don't Become Shackled with Stuff

My friend lost it all. Hurricanes Katrina and Rita wiped him out. As he lamented his plight to his daughter, she brought him back to reality with a simple statement: "Daddy, it's just stuff." That was all he needed to hear to remember not to become shackled by things.

Jesus wants to free us from slavery to things. He said, "Do not worry about your life, what you will eat or drink; or about your body, what you will wear" (Matthew 6:25, NIV). On another occasion, He said, "A man's life does not consist in the abundance of his possessions" (Luke 12:15, NIV).

As I sat in the U.S. Senate restaurant, I noticed a multimillionaire senator seated to my right, ordering from the same menu. There are no $50,000 omelets. Not much is needed to eliminate want in life. Perhaps this is why the apostle Paul advised, "Having food and clothing, be satisfied" (1 Timothy 6:8).

Refuse to Put Earthly Gain above Heavenly Investments

In Matthew 6, Jesus gives further guidance about winning over worry: "Do not store up for yourselves treasures on earth. . . . But store up for yourselves treasures in heaven" (Matthew 6:19-20, NIV). He encouraged people not to put earthly gain above heavenly investments.

One of the best investments my mother ever made was providing a Christian education for all her children, even though my family had little money. My mother made an investment in eternity.

How are you investing in eternity? Often we can't win over worry until our priorities shift from earthly concerns to heavenly ones: feeding the hungry, clothing the naked, visiting the sick, ministering to the incarcerated, and giving hospitality to strangers (Matthew 25:31-46). Placing heavenly priorities before earthly gain is the best investment, often exposing us to needs that dwarf our own.

Imitate the Animals

"Look at the birds of the air," said Jesus. "They do not sow or reap or store away in barns, and yet your heavenly Father feeds them. Are you not much more valuable than they?" (Matthew 6:26, NIV). The animals have much to teach us about worry-free living. They aren't free-choice agents like humans, but they obey their Creator.

During a famine in Israel, God spoke to the prophet Elijah and told him to go to a brook at Kerith because "I have commanded the ravens to feed you there" (1 Kings 17:4, NKJV). God commanded birds to feed His servant during a difficult time. The animals had no choice; they must obey God. A homing pigeon has no choice but to go home.

Those who seek to win over worry would do well to imitate the animals. They obey God because they can't do otherwise. How much better for us who have the choice to obey God's commands as revealed in Scripture! We should learn from the animals.

See the Pointlessness of Worry

Worry is often pointless; most of the things I have worried about have never happened. Jesus alluded to the pointlessness of worry when He said, "Who of you by worrying can add a single hour to his life?" (Matthew 6:27, NIV).

Samson's parents forgot that worrying is pointless. They were distraught because their son lustfully pursued Philistine women (Judges 14). They reminded him that he should marry an Israelite girl, but he insisted on having his way. They continued to worry, not realizing a very important fact: God was behind Samson's wandering, because He wanted to find occasion against the Philistines (Judges 14:4). Samson's parents worried pointlessly about something that God would use for His glory.

Trust God for Lesser Things

Jesus encourages us to win over worry by trusting God for life's lesser things. If God can control the galaxies, why don't we think He can take care of our smaller concerns? Jesus said, "See how the lilies of the field grow. They do not labor or spin. Yet I tell you that not even Solomon in all his splendor was dressed like one of these" (Matthew 6:28-29, NIV).

After visiting an art exhibition called "Bodies," I was overwhelmed by God's design of the human body. This exhibition showed the circulatory, respiratory, digestive, and reproductive systems, isolating them so that their nuanced complexity could be better appreciated. When I finished looking, I was ready to worship. I agreed with the psalmist that we are "fearfully and wonderfully made" (Psalm 139:14, NIV).

If we were walking in the woods and came across a basketball, I could assume that someone had been there. The presence of the ball would indicate human activity. Similarly, the significant evidence I see for God all around me helps me to trust Him to take care even of life's less daunting concerns. Trusting Him for lesser things enables me to manage worry.

Expect God to Meet Your Needs

Jesus promises that God will take care of our needs (Matthew 6:31-32). This theme is reiterated in Philippians 4:19: "My God shall supply every need of yours, according to His riches in Christ Jesus." We can win over worry by claiming God's promise to supply all of our needs.

This realization brings serenity. When something is missing in my life, the Lord reassures me it's not something I need now. If I did, He would supply it. Unfortunately, we often mistake our wants for needs. But God has promised to cover the basics, to supply our needs, so why worry?

Seek God's Will First

Jesus ended His lecture on winning over worry by suggesting we first seek God's will. He said, "But seek first his kingdom and his righteousness, and all these things will be given to you as well" (Matthew 6:33, NIV). In short, put first things first. To seek God's Kingdom first means making His will our first priority.

Moses had his priorities right. Hebrews 11:25 says, "He chose rather to suffer afflictions with God's people than to enjoy the pleasures of sin for a season." This was an amazing choice. Had Moses continued on the track his foster family intended, he probably would have eventually become Pharaoh, considered a deity by the Egyptians. Instead, he took the less-traveled road of fidelity to God's will, putting first things first.

Live One Day at a Time

Finally, live one day at a time. "Therefore do not worry about tomorrow, for tomorrow will worry about itself. Each day has enough trouble of its own" (Matthew 6:34, NIV). Jesus didn't teach us to pray, "Give us this week our weekly bread." We should live in day-tight compartments, not worrying about what the next sunrise will bring. This is suggested in Deuteronomy 33:25: "As your days, so shall your strength be" (NKJV).

The hymn "I Know Who Holds Tomorrow," by Ira Stanphill, captures this sentiment better than most:

> *I don't know about tomorrow,*
> *I just live from day to day.*
> *I don't borrow from its sunshine,*
> *For its skies may turn to gray.*
> *I don't worry o'er the future,*
> *For I know what Jesus said,*
> *And today I'll walk beside Him,*
> *For He knows what is ahead.*[14]

AN ACTION PLAN TO HELP YOU WIN OVER WORRY

> *Don't become shackled with stuff.*

> *Refuse to put earthly gain above heavenly investments.*

> *Imitate the animals.*

> *See the pointlessness of worry.*

> *Trust God for lesser things.*

> *Expect God to meet your needs.*

> *Seek God's will first.*

> *Live one day at a time.*

19

FIND GAIN IN YOUR PAIN

THE PHONE RANG, and I picked it up. "Blacks' residence."

The voice on the other end sounded animated. "Hi, Barry, this is Michael, and have I got a deal for you."

The deal involved work; he wanted me to write a sermon, titled "The Last Sermon," to be included in a book that would be a spin-off of Randy Pausch's best seller, *The Last Lecture*. In his popular book, Pausch, a computer science professor at Carnegie Mellon University, expanded on a lecture he had given at the school in which he was asked to pretend he was delivering his final lecture to his students before dying. What would he say to them? What advice would he give?

As Pausch prepared the lecture, he received a terminal diagnosis of pancreatic cancer, which would take his life within a year. Suddenly, the hypothetical had become reality. No longer was he pretending; this probably would be his last opportunity to impart wisdom to the next generation. His last lecture, which became a

YouTube phenomenon seen by millions, took on much greater significance.

Now Michael was asking me to do something similar—to prepare my final sermon, the one I would preach if I were dying.

As I thought about the proposed book and the excitement in Michael's voice, I said to myself, "I wonder what Jesus said during His last lecture or sermon. I guess it's time to find out."

Picking up my Bible, I opened to John 16—the beginning of Christ's farewell discourse to His disciples in the upper room. In His "last lecture," Jesus provided His followers with a reality check as He delivered news—both good and bad—that was intended to empower them to effectively face opposition for His name's sake. "I've got bad news for you," He said to His disciples. "People will persecute you and attempt to kill you. When they do this, many will think they are doing God's will. I must also tell you that I'm leaving. I must go away.

"I also have some good news. After My departure, I will send you another Comforter, the Holy Spirit, who will lead and guide you into all truth." Concluding this final lecture, He declared, "I'm telling you these things so that you might have peace. In this world, you'll have pressure. Take courage, for I have overcome the world" (John 16:33).

"That's it!" I almost shouted. "I'll preach my hypothetical last sermon by using the same theme Jesus emphasized in His last lecture: facing life's pressures and opposition with courage."

Trust God's Providential Leading

Daniel 2 records an interesting story about a king who had a troubling dream that he couldn't remember. He called his wise men together and said, "Tell me the dream I've forgotten."

"King," they responded, "simply tell us the dream, and we'll give you the interpretation."

It didn't take a genius IQ for King Nebuchadnezzar to realize that his wise men had been deceiving him about their abilities. "All of the wise men and their families will die," he decreed.

Fortunately, Daniel and his friends belonged to the profession of wise men and weren't phonies. "Give us a little time," said Daniel, "and we will reveal what the king dreamed and the interpretation of the dream."

The king gave Daniel this requested time, and soon Daniel stood before him with this revelation: "King, you saw a large image whose parts were made of different metals: the head of gold, chest of silver, belly of bronze, and legs of iron. The feet were a mixture of iron and clay."

"That's exactly what I saw!" cried the king.

"You saw something else," continued Daniel. "You beheld a stone emerge from the mountain and smite the image's base, destroying it. That stone began to grow until it filled the earth." Daniel then proceeded to interpret the dream, telling the monarch that Babylon was the head of gold that would be followed by a succession of kingdoms of lesser glory, eventually leading to the climax of human history. At that climax, the God of Heaven would set up a Kingdom that shall never be destroyed (Daniel 2).

Finding blessing in adversity involves believing that God's power extends over earthly rulers and circumstances, as Nebuchadnezzar learned. This confidence comes from trusting God's sovereign providence, for He is in control of human history. He is never surprised by the variety of events that occur in our world, for "in everything He is working for the good of those who love Him" (Romans 8:28).

In Mark 4, Jesus' disciples battle a raging tempest while Jesus sleeps in the stern of the boat. When all seems lost, they turn to their Master for help. He rises and says to the storm, "Peace, be still!" (Mark 4:39, NKJV), and the winds and the waves obey Him. Turning to His disciples, He asks them a strange question: "Why were you fearful?"

"Pardon me, Lord," I would have responded. "I can think of several good reasons for our fear. We've swallowed water; our bodies have been drenched by the sea. The boat is filling with water, as the bottomless sea beckons." But Jesus' question is a reminder that He expects His disciples to believe that His power extends over everything—which is the meaning of omnipotence. Even in the face of tragedy, we must learn to say, "It is well with my soul," as songwriter Horatio Spafford did when he penned his famous hymn after losing his four daughters in a maritime accident.

Ignore the Opposition

David teaches us what to do with some of the opposition we face as we seek to turn life's pains into gains. Arriving on the battlefield, as recorded in 1 Samuel 17, David heard the giant Goliath threaten Israel and insult God. David asked, "Who is this uncircumcised Philistine that he should cry out against the armies of the living God?" This question elicited immediate opposition from David's brother Eliab.

"'What are you doing around here anyway?' he demanded. 'What about those few sheep you're supposed to be taking care of? I know about your pride and deceit. You just want to see the battle!'" (1 Samuel 17:28, NLT).

David responded, "What have I done now?" but for the most part, he ignored the opposition and continued his quest to restore God's honor on the battlefield.

In Nehemiah 4:1-6, Nehemiah faces opposition from Sanballat and Tobiah as he seeks to rebuild the walls of Jerusalem. These enemies try to distract and discourage Nehemiah, but he ignores them and continues to build, completing what seemed an impossible task in only fifty-two days. To turn life's pains into gains, sometimes you must ignore the opposition.

When Jesus stood before Pilate, He ignored the opposition. He uttered so few words that Pilate finally declared, "Why don't You say something? Don't You know I have the power to have You killed or to set You free?"

Jesus responded, "You would have no power over Me except it were given you from above" (John 19:11). Our Lord didn't say much to Pilate because it wouldn't have helped the situation. He once said, "Don't give what is holy to the dog, and don't cast your pearls before swine" (Matthew 7:6). With Pilate, He was simply practicing what He preached, ignoring unworthy opposition.

Do you ignore opposition when necessary? If you need to face opposition head-on, then do so with courage; but don't waste valuable time and energy chasing your detractors. Focus instead on the movement of God's sovereign providence, as you watch Him open doors that no enemy can shut.

Fast and Pray

In Mark 9, Jesus' disciples unsuccessfully attempt to cast out a demon from a possessed boy, whose father had brought him to them. Their failure provides ammunition to Jesus' critics, who say to Him, "We brought this demon-possessed boy to Your disciples, and they couldn't cast out the demons."

Quickly, Jesus did what His disciples had failed to do and exorcised the demon. This prompted His disciples, when they were alone with Jesus later, to ask, "Lord, why couldn't we cast out the demon?"

Jesus answered, "This kind comes out but by fasting and prayer."

To face opposition with courage, wield the spiritual weapons of fasting and prayer, a dynamic combination. Fasting adds energy to our prayers because it is an indicator of intensity. And intensity counts. James 5:16 says that "the earnest prayers of the righteous have great power." And when we want something from God so much that we stop eating, amazing power is often unleashed.

My middle son, Brendan, earned academic scholarships to several fine universities. Unfortunately, he didn't want to attend any of them. "Dad and Mom," he pleaded, "I want to go to Yale." Well, Yale didn't offer merit scholarships, only ones based on financial need, for which Brendan didn't qualify.

"Son," I insisted, "Yale is $43,000 a year. Please accept one of the scholarships, and your mother and I will pay for your medical school."

"But, Dad, I want to go to Yale," he whispered.

"If you accept one of the scholarships," I bargained, "I'll buy you a new car."

"But, Dad, I want to go to Yale."

His mother and I ended up paying for Yale tuition because my son earnestly desired to go there.

In Luke 11:13, Jesus says, "If you then, being evil, know how to give good gifts to your children, how much more will your heavenly Father give the Holy Spirit to those who ask Him!" (NKJV). If the earnest petitions of my son moved my hand to my wallet, how much more will our earnest supplications to our heavenly Father bring us wonderful blessings from His bountiful riches?

Strive to Live a Holy Life

How would you feel if you knew you had only a few days to live? King Hezekiah was devastated when the prophet Isaiah informed him that God had said, "Set your house in order, for you shall die and not live" (Isaiah 38:1, NKJV). This wasn't the news the sick monarch wanted to hear.

But Hezekiah knew something about the power of holiness. Turning his face to the wall, he poured out this passionate prayer to God: "Remember, O Lord, how I have always tried to be faithful to You and to do what is pleasing in Your sight" (Isaiah 38:3). Then he began to weep bitterly.

God heard his prayer and saw his tears. Before the prophet Isaiah could leave the palace, God said to him, "Go back and tell the king, I have heard him and will extend his life fifteen more years."

In order to face opposition with courage, we must strive to live a holy life. Hezekiah made his efforts to please God the bargaining chip in his prayer, realizing the truth of Psalm 5:12: "The righteous are surrounded with the shield of God's favor."

This doesn't mean we're saved by works. But even as our obedient children will receive things from us that our rebellious offspring will not, embracing holiness brings added blessings from God. As Psalm 84:11 puts it, "No good thing will God withhold from the upright."

Develop a Bias for Action

During my teenage years, I fell and chipped a tooth. In the inner city, that usually meant living with a broken tooth, for dental visits were rare. For years, I flashed my damaged smile, through high school and college and beyond. Finally, when I was serving as a pastor in North Carolina, a church member spoke to me one Sunday as he was leaving the service. "Pastor, you know it's possible to fix your tooth. I'm a dentist. Come by my office and, for no charge, I'll repair that chipped tooth." I did and soon flashed my new smile with confidence.

Afterward, finding myself alone, I began meditating about why it had taken me so long to do something about my tooth. The repairs took only a few minutes, yet I had to be nudged by a member of my church before I took the simple and inexpensive step to rehabilitate my appearance. Inaction can be dangerous when we're facing opposition. We must develop an inclination for action if we're to face life's opposition with courage.

Find Allies

But don't try to face life's opposition on your own; find allies. After the Flood, as the sons of Noah and their descendants began to repopulate the earth, the people who settled in the land of Shinar decided to prepare for the next disaster by building a tower to heaven (Genesis 11:1-4). They labored together, building a ziggurat that stretched toward the sky. Then God said, "Let Us go down and confound their language, for humanity united can accomplish anything" (Genesis 11:7). And God did exactly that, confusing the people by changing their one language into many.

If humanity united for evil can accomplish the impossible, so can people united for good. That is why those who want to face opposition with courage should find allies. Ecclesiastes 4:12 says, "A person standing alone can be attacked and defeated, but two can stand back-to-back and conquer. Three are even better, for a triple-braided cord is not easily broken" (NLT).

How can this be true? It seems that if one can chase a thousand, two should be able to chase two thousand. But it's different with God's mathematics. When good people unite, it creates a synergy that makes the resulting force greater than the sum of its parts.

We see this with David and Jonathan. Jonathan, heir to Israel's throne, helped save David's life (1 Samuel 20). Jonathan's father, King Saul, wanted to kill David because he saw him as a rival to the throne. But Jonathan monitored his father's homicidal intentions, warning David and saving his life, even though it meant that Jonathan would not succeed to his father's throne. David found an ally in the king's son, and what a difference it made! Find allies and you will be able to deal with life's opposition more effectively.

Develop a Resolute Mind

Each year, many people make New Year's resolutions, only to discover they lack the power of resolve. They lack the passion required to accomplish their goals.

In Esther 4, the queen of Persia and Media, an Israelite, learned that her people had been targeted for extermination. Her uncle Mordecai informed her of the plot, warning her that she must act. Esther said, "Tell my uncle to fast and pray with the people for three days, and I'll do the same with my maidens. Then I'll go to the king to try to solve this problem, and if I perish, I perish" (Esther 4:16).

Wow! "If I perish, I perish." Now that's a resolute mind. It sounds similar to what Job said when he declared about God, "Though he slay me, yet will I trust in him" (Job 13:15, KJV).

In His farewell discourse, Jesus warned His disciples that they would face pressure and opposition in this world (John 16:33). You and I can courageously face opposition by putting our trust in God.

AN ACTION PLAN TO HELP YOU FIND GAIN IN YOUR PAIN

> *Trust God's providential leading.*

> *Ignore the opposition.*

> *Fast and pray.*

> *Strive to live a holy life.*

> *Develop a bias for action.*

> *Find allies.*

> *Develop a resolute mind.*

20

ENDURE THE TEST

WHAT GOOD GIFTS have you received from God? In James 1:17, we're reminded of the source of all gifts: "Every good and perfect gift is from above, coming down from the Father of the heavenly lights, who does not change like shifting shadows" (NIV). That's right. All the good in your life comes from one source: God. It would be good to remind yourself regularly of how God has blessed you. He wakes you each morning, lending you heartbeats for the day. He gives you air to breathe, food and water for sustenance, and friends to nurture your spirit. Make a habit of thanking God for His blessings.

Cultivate an Attitude of Gratitude
Cultivating an attitude of gratitude provides you with the power to endure life's tests and strengthens you to follow Jesus' example of gratefulness. Jesus filled His life with gratitude. Before feeding the five thousand or resurrecting Lazarus or leaving the upper

room for Calvary, He gave thanks to His Father (John 6, 11; Matthew 26). If Jesus could sing praises to God as He headed to Calvary, we have no excuse for failing to bless the Lord at all times and keeping praises continually on our lips (Psalm 34:1).

Cultivating an attitude of gratitude means being ready to thank God even when facing hardships. Daniel provides an example of how to do this. He faced death in a lion's den after the king was tricked into signing a foolish decree that Daniel then violated. "Now when Daniel learned that the decree had been published, he went home to his upstairs room where the windows opened toward Jerusalem. Three times a day he got down on his knees and prayed, giving thanks to his God, just as he had done before" (Daniel 6:10, NIV).

This is amazing. Daniel prayed with gratitude when it was illegal to do so. He prayed when prayer meant risking death at the jaws of ravenous lions. Daniel shows us how to endure life's trials by living with gratitude.

Isn't it wonderful how God equips His children for the doors He opens? This is a blessing that should engender gratitude. Throughout human history, God has given abilities to His children that enabled them to maximize their opportunities. Joseph and Daniel could interpret dreams. Esther possessed the gift of beauty, and Samson was given extraordinary strength. David was given abilities as a warrior and musician, and his son Solomon was supplied with the gift of wisdom.

The God who blessed those who lived before our time is still in the blessing business, continuing to supply us with the abilities we need to make a positive difference in our world. We should give thanks for His goodness.

How often do you thank God? When your life is filled with pain, do you still give thanks to God? If you follow the examples of Jesus and Daniel, you will express gratitude to God regardless of your circumstances.

Be Tenacious

When going through life's tests, have you ever wondered if it's worth persevering? After all, what's in it for you? When you learn to anticipate God's reward for your faithfulness, it becomes easier to endure life's tribulations. James encourages us in this way: "Blessed is the man who perseveres under trial, because when he has stood the test, he will receive the crown of life that God has promised to those who love him" (James 1:12, NIV).

This is a wonderful Bible verse. It shows us that God wants us to anticipate His rewards. Once Peter said to Jesus, "Lord, we have left all to follow You. What are we going to get for our sacrifices?" (Matthew 19:27). Jesus didn't condemn Peter for being interested in rewards. He didn't suggest it was unspiritual to expect to receive something because of sacrifices. What did Jesus say? He told Peter, "Everyone who has left father and mother, houses and land will receive in this life one hundred times as much and in the world to come eternal life" (Matthew 19:29). Jesus wants to encourage us with the expectation of rewards.

The apostle Paul faced a martyr's death with the expectation of a reward. In writing to his protégé Timothy, he said, "I have fought a good fight, I have finished my course, I have kept the faith" (2 Timothy 4:7, KJV). But Paul continued, "Henceforth there is laid up for me a crown of righteousness, which the Lord, the righteous judge, shall give me at that day" (2 Timothy 4:8, KJV). Do you think God would talk so much about heaven if He didn't want us to be motivated by rewards? He desires to give good gifts to His children and to encourage them to persevere. Through Paul, in Galatians 6:9, He reminds us that a certain harvest will come to those who don't stop doing good for His Kingdom, even though the task can be wearying. As you anticipate your reward, know that eternal life is a part of the package (John 3:16).

Don't Blame God

When tested, whom should you blame? Don't blame God! "When tempted, no one should say, 'God is tempting me.' For God cannot be tempted by evil, nor does he tempt anyone" (James 1:13, NIV). God isn't the source of your test or temptation. His plan is to give you a future and a hope, to bring you to a desired destination (Jeremiah 29:11-13).

So what is the root of your test? James 1:14 provides the answer: "We are tempted when, by our own evil desires, we are dragged away and enticed." The root is our own evil desires. You see, we're born in sin and shaped in iniquity (Psalm 51:5), and our sorry inheritance is the propensity to do evil. We have a flammable area in our hearts that can be ignited by testing and temptation. My flammable area may be different from yours, for our besetting sins may differ (Hebrews 12:1). Nonetheless, each of us has a sin nature that leads us toward transgressions. We're born this way; hence the need for a new birth (John 3).

This new birth does not mean that we will no longer encounter testing. Throughout the seasons of our existence, we will continue to be pulled by sinful urges and desires. One such test comes from a desire for riches: "People who want to get rich fall into temptation and a trap and into many foolish and harmful desires that plunge men into ruin and destruction" (1 Timothy 6:9, NIV). We've all heard what some people will do to get money—steal from family members, prostitute themselves, and even rob God (Malachi 3:8). They succumb to many temptations in their efforts to acquire more wealth.

Think of it. One of the reasons Judas betrayed Jesus was for money.

He turned his master over to the enemy for thirty pieces of silver (Matthew 26:15). This was a significant sum, more than four months' wages for a common laborer, or enough to buy a field—which is what happened with Judas's blood money after he tried unsuccessfully to return it and then hanged himself (Matthew 27:3-10).

Money isn't all that may test us. In the story of the farmer who scattered seeds over four kinds of soil, one portion of ground was filled with thorns that eventually choked the growing plants. Jesus explained to His disciples what these thorns represent: "the worries of this life and the deceitfulness of wealth" (Matthew 13:22, NIV). So we can add worry to the list of things that can test us.

During my twenty-seven-year military career, I spent more time than I should have worrying about promotions. On most workdays, something would happen that would prompt me to ponder my future possibilities for upward mobility. I wasted valuable time and energy worrying, when 90 percent of the things I concerned myself about never happened. I discovered in time the uselessness of worry. Don't permit your worries to test you unnecessarily.

Remember the Wages of Sin

To endure life's tests, it's important to remember the results of continually giving in to sin. James 1:15 reminds us of sin's ultimate goal: "After desire has conceived, it gives birth to sin; and sin, when it is full-grown, gives birth to death" (NIV). When we continue in sin, it eventually leads to death.

This is an important insight. Whenever you're faced with a temptation, remember its ultimate aim—death. It's like a game of chess in which each player seeks to checkmate the other's king. The devil seeks to checkmate us. The Bible describes him as a "roaring lion, seeking whom he may devour" (1 Peter 5:8, NKJV). Those who want to avoid sin's final destination must endure temptation and testing.

By keeping the ultimate outcome of sin in mind, we can see how foolish it is to envy sinners (Proverbs 23:17). The Bible says they will be cut off (Psalm 37:2) and destroyed (Isaiah 1:28). How often have we seen reports about someone living in the proverbial fast lane who has come to an untimely and premature death? We read about star athletes who are shot in strip clubs or who crash while driving intoxicated. We read about drug overdoses and health complications from steroid use. The knowledge that sin, though pleasurable, is an enemy, not a friend, will provide the wisdom we need to endure life's tests.

America went through a gangster period, during which names such as Al Capone, Baby Face Nelson, and Machine Gun Kelly dominated the headlines. This was the Bonnie and Clyde period of our history. But these legendary figures usually came to unflattering ends, for "the way of the transgressor is hard" (Proverbs 13:15, ASV).

Do you sometimes find yourself wishing you could live the lifestyle of the fast-lane crowd? Don't indulge those wishes. Instead, remember that God places prohibitions in our lives to protect us and to enable us to live with true abundance. Trust His process and endure your tests.

Help Others through Their Trials

Once you've endured your tests, be prepared to help others get through their challenges. One great way to do this is to share your good news. Often one of the most helpful things you can do for someone facing trials is to tell them about difficulties that God helped you to endure.

Isn't this what Naaman's maid did? She was a prisoner of war with her own problems, serving in the household of a Syrian general (2 Kings 5). But having accepted her plight, enduring the test, she turned her concern to the pain in her master's house, for Naaman was ill, dying of dreaded leprosy. This maid said to her mistress, "If only my master would see the prophet who is in Samaria! He would cure him of his leprosy!" (2 Kings 5:3, NIV). She shared her good news.

She could have had a very different attitude, actually rejoicing that this enemy soldier was dying. She could have resented being a slave in his home and prayed that he and his nation would receive divine retribution. She could have seen his leprosy as a judgment from God. But she didn't do any of these things. Instead, she sought to help him, to share good news that would bring abundance to his house.

After World War II, America helped Europe recover from the ravages of war with the Marshall Plan. This initiative used American wealth to help rebuild Europe, and was named for then Secretary of State George Marshall. Through this plan, America provided good news to nations bludgeoned by war. This was one of the finest humanitarian acts in American history.

Do you hoard your blessings or share them with others? When God has blessed you and enabled you to endure life's tests, follow the example of Naaman's maid and share your good news with those who need to hear it. You can be like Philip, who explained the Bible to an Ethiopian eunuch and led him to Christ (Acts 8). You can be God's instrument for comfort in these challenging times. Seeing the gain that your pain can bring into the lives of others will inspire you to continue to endure future hardships.

AN ACTION PLAN TO HELP YOU ENDURE THE TEST

> *Cultivate an attitude of gratitude.*

> *Be tenacious.*

> *Don't blame God.*
> *Remember the wages of sin.*
> *Help others through their trials.*

21

GAIN BY LOSING

GENEROSITY ENABLES US to manage life's crises, empowering us to gain by losing. In 1 Kings 17:9, God says to Elijah the prophet: "Leave this dry brook and go to Zarephath in Sidon. I have commanded a widow there to feed you." This woman, of the same race and religion as the wicked Queen Jezebel, had heard the voice of God and obeyed by sharing what she thought was her last meal with a hungry prophet. Because of her obedience, God rewarded her with a continuous supply of food until the famine ceased. Her generosity provided her with a gain she would have missed had she refused to sacrifice what she had. She found a blessing in her adversity through generosity.

Many years later, Jesus commented about this woman's faith: "There were many widows in Israel at the time of Elijah the prophet," He observed. "But God sent him to the widow of Zarephath" (Luke 4:25-26). Could it be that no Israelite widows possessed sufficient faith or generosity to gain by losing?

First, generosity enables us to gain by losing because it implements the unstoppable laws of sowing and reaping. Seedtime and harvest will continue as long as the earth revolves (Genesis 8:22), and generosity is one way to plant seeds that yield a bountiful harvest. Inevitably, we reap more than we sow, thirtyfold, sixtyfold, one-hundredfold (Mark 4:8). Little did this widow dream that God would use her sacrificial giving to save her and her child from starvation. She reaped an abundant harvest indeed.

Jesus once said, "Those who seek to save their lives shall lose them. But those who lose their lives for My sake will find them" (Luke 17:33). Few acts of generosity are greater than losing your life. This refers to martyrdom, but also to investing our lives in something greater than ourselves. In other words, find something worth dying for if you want to be fit to live. Giving one's life in generous service to others is a sure way to gain by losing and to turn life's setbacks into stepping-stones.

Another reason generosity enables us to gain by losing is that it reflects a divine maxim found in Acts 20:35: "It is more blessed to give than to receive." When the Good Samaritan, in Jesus' parable, risked his life in generously helping a wounded Jew on the Jericho road, Jesus celebrated the man's actions as an example of true neighborliness (Luke 10).

There is someone else whom Jesus celebrated—Mary of Bethany (John 12). Six days before the Passover, with the shadow of the Cross now falling across His path, Jesus, along with His disciples, made His way back to Bethany, where He had often basked in the sunshine of His warm friendship with Mary, Martha, and Lazarus. Entering their home, He smelled the aroma of Martha's superb cooking and nodded toward the smiling Lazarus, recently resurrected from the dead. With special affection, He gave Mary a quick embrace. In minutes, dinner was served.

As they ate, Mary took an expensive bottle of perfume and poured it on Jesus' feet. The sweet, almost intoxicating fragrance filled the room, igniting a stir of conversation and controversy. Finally, Judas spoke for the group. He asked, "Why the waste? Why wasn't this perfume sold for 300 silver coins and the money given to the poor?"

A hush fell over the room, but Jesus broke the silence by defending and celebrating Mary's generosity. "Leave her alone," He said with uncharacteristic sternness. "She has kept this perfume for the day of My burial. You'll always have the poor with you, but you won't always have Me!" Jesus publicly confronted Judas and defended His friend, who was willing to gain by losing. He said of Mary, "And wherever the Gospel is preached, the story of Mary's generosity will be told" (Matthew 26:13).

Mary's generosity enabled her to find blessing in adversity. What was her adversity? She knew that Jesus was going to die. By sitting at His feet during His visits, she had developed a greater theological sophistication than even Jesus' twelve disciples. While they jockeyed for position in an earthly kingdom, desiring the chief seats, Mary's heart turned toward Calvary. Her desire to honor her Lord before His death enabled her to be absent at the tomb on Easter Sunday. That's right. Mary of Bethany was not at the garden tomb on Easter, having already anointed her Savior's body. She had prepared herself for the difficulty of losing Him and had gained by losing.

The secular outlook reverses the maxim of gaining by losing, declaring it more blessed to receive than to give. This is, however, contrary to numerous examples in history and Scripture. History is kindest to givers, not takers. For example, rarely does anyone ask about the financial worth of Roosevelt or Churchill or Gandhi or King. What these givers contributed to humanity's well-being was worth much more than money.

Similarly, when her people were threatened with genocide, Esther sacrificed her life to inform King Xerxes about Haman's nefarious plot to slaughter the Jews, thereby gaining from imminent loss and turning adversity into advantage. And Ruth became one of Jesus' ancestors because she generously refused to leave Naomi during a season of great grief. We remember Hannah's great gain after she gave Israel a great prophet by generously returning her son for service in the Tabernacle. Repeatedly, history and sacred literature demonstrate the efficacy of generous giving.

Third, generosity enables us to gain by losing because it softens and mitigates the pain in our world. Whatever crisis you must endure, focus on giving and make the world better. When you make the world better, you create a more positive environment in which your crisis can be resolved.

In 1 Samuel 30, David pursues the Amalekites in an effort to regain what his enemies have stolen. God had already assured the young David that he would recover everything the enemy had taken, so he pursued his foes with great optimism. On the way to his rendezvous with success, he encountered a dying Egyptian servant and stopped to help him. This generous act yielded David valuable information and guidance, enabling him to defeat his enemies. During one of his life's lowest points, David gained by giving generously. By helping the less fortunate, he made the world a safer place to manage his crisis.

It is not only possible but necessary for us to gain by losing, for it makes us more like God. The Bible challenges us to strive for perfection, "even as your Father in heaven is perfect" (Matthew 5:48, NLT). One critical part of God's perfection is His generosity. As we look at the varied beauty of creation, with its colors and majesty, God's generosity is clearly visible. The closer we get to God and the more we become like Him, the more generous we will become. Indeed, God managed the crisis of evil by giving. His plan to save humanity is an amazing example of celestial generosity.

How can we give like God? First, we should give our all. God gave His Son, a gift beyond anything else heaven could give. Second, we should give with a focus on human needs. "I have not come to call the righteous," admonished Jesus, "but sinners to repentance" (Luke 5:32, NIV). In Matthew 25, we are reminded that God will judge our generosity by how we feed the hungry, clothe the naked, care for strangers, help the sick, and minister to the incarcerated. In Luke 4, Jesus says that His ministry seeks to deliver captives, restore sight to the blind, and comfort the oppressed. We give like God when we target the lost, the lonely, and the least. We give like Him when we give gratefully, passionately, promptly, wisely, and dangerously.

Give Gratefully

Gratitude should be our greatest motivation for giving. It certainly was a force in Joseph's life. When he explained to Potiphar's wife his reasons for resisting her overtures, he spoke gratefully of God's blessings. Because he had received God's generosity, Joseph refused to engage in sin. Similarly, Mary of Bethany's gratitude prompted her generosity. Jesus defended her by explaining that she wanted to do something special for Him because she was grateful.

When gratitude provides the foundation of our gifts, we obey the mandate of 2 Corinthians 9:7 to "give not grudgingly or of necessity, but cheerfully." One of my dear friends, Wintley Phipps, a great gospel singer, told me of a time when he was traveling first-class on an airplane and heard a voice. "Wintley," the voice whispered, "how would you like to live this lifestyle for the rest of your life? I can make it happen for you, and much more, if you'll only stop singing about Jesus." My friend knew this was not God's voice. He had made a commitment to sing for Christ, but now demonic forces sought to woo him away.

As he thought about the goodness of God and the generous gifts he had received, Wintley wrote, as a gift to God, the song "I Give You My Life." Gratitude is a laudable and powerful motivation for cheerfully giving to God and humanity.

Give Passionately

Mary of Bethany also gave passionately. When she anointed the head and feet of her Lord, and then used her hair to dry His feet, this was not a casual acknowledgment of what Christ meant to her. This was a woman passionately saying good-bye and thank you to the center of her life.

We see a similar passion from Hannah in 1 Samuel 1. She had prayed so fervently for a child that Eli the priest thought she was drunk. When he learned it was her anguish and travail that had pushed her to such intense prayer, he told her that God would give her what she had requested.

When God did His part and gave her a son, Hannah kept her promise. She had told God that her response to His generous gift would be to permit her child to be raised in His house. After Samuel was weaned, Hannah made her way back to the Tabernacle to deliver her son to the priest. He would be reared in the Tabernacle, becoming one of Israel's great prophets, for his mother had given passionately.

Give Promptly

We should not delay in our giving. Thank God that Mary of Bethany gave promptly! Had she waited, Jesus would have passed through Gethsemane on His way to Calvary, and she would not have had a second chance to give her Master this gift. How she must have consoled herself after His death, glad that at least she had been able to give Him sweet fragrances before He suffered.

Many fail to gain by losing because they give too late. Sometimes in life delayed obedience is disobedience. We can be like the five foolish virgins in Matthew 25, who didn't purchase their oil in time to meet the bridegroom.

Some try to love their children after years of being distracted by their work, only to discover that the children have become too busy for their tardy attentiveness. Harry Chapin's 1974 hit song "Cat's in the Cradle" describes a father who didn't have time to spend with his son until it was too late—the boy had grown up to be just like the dad, with no time to bond and nurture.

I once saw a television program in which a journalist interviewed the senior President Bush and his wife, Barbara. "What do you two give each other for birthday presents?" the reporter queried.

"Oh, we don't give birthday presents anymore," Mrs. Bush responded quickly. "Anything I want, George gets me anyway, or I can buy it myself." Then turning to the reporter she asked with a sweep of her hand, "Do you see anything in this room that you want? As old as we are, we're in the business of giving things away."

The Lebanese-American poet and mystic Kahlil Gibran once said, "One day all that you have will be given. So give now, that the season of giving will be yours and not your inheritors." That's a good commitment to make to yourself. Give while you can still see the recipients' smiles and hear their joyous words of gratitude.

One of the great joys of my life came when God gave me the opportunity to help my mother purchase a home. She had made so many sacrifices for my siblings and me throughout our lives that my gift seemed small. Mama was grateful and often expressed to me how much she enjoyed living in her house. Little did we know that she would not live much longer, her life prematurely shortened by a medical mistake. But in our last conversation, she again expressed her gratitude for my gift.

At her funeral, these words were still fresh in my mind, and I thanked God that I had not delayed in giving. The adversity of her death was mitigated by the memory of having blessed her through giving.

Give Wisely

Mary's gift was also given wisely. It was intended to encourage Jesus during the most difficult season of His life, enabling Him to stay focused on the advantage in His adversity. As He hung on the cross, He knew that most of His disciples had fled. Religious leaders cursed Him, and the multitude screamed for His death. Though He felt forsaken by God and humanity, He still must have seen at least one point of light in the darkness. After all, Mary of Bethany had been an apt pupil. She had anticipated His anguish a few days before with her expensive gift and had blessed Him with her wise generosity.

How wise are you in your giving? Do you throw good money after bad? Once I was walking with a minister friend through Union Square in Washington, DC. The poor and the needy with outstretched hands pleaded for money as we passed by. My friend continued walking, and I wondered how he could seemingly ignore the cries of society's marginalized. The plea of one beggar in particular seemed pointed and piteous. "Mister, I'm hungry. Could you please spare some change so I can get something to eat?"

Ignoring this cry, I followed my friend into the train station, where he stopped at a sandwich shop. He purchased several sandwiches, placing them in a large bag. Then, turning to me, he said,

"Come on, we've got work to do." We returned to the open square, where the beggars continued lifting their voices for help. My friend asked for my assistance as he gave fresh, delicious sandwiches to the hungry.

He had given wisely. Had he given his money to anyone who asked, he couldn't be certain how they would spend it. And while there are times when such giving is quite appropriate, we must be good stewards of the resources God has given us. This means giving to others in a way that will empower and bless them.

A senator friend of mine is fond of telling a story about a village with an unusual problem. People kept falling off a steep cliff nearby. Several fell to the bottom and received injuries. A few even died. The village's medical establishment responded to this challenge by positioning an ambulance fleet at the base of the cliff, to immediately rush those who had fallen to modern hospitals for treatment.

It occurred to some people, however, that a wiser course might be to build a fence at the top of the cliff to prevent people from falling in the first place. When they voiced this idea, they were ignored, and no fence was built.

But as people kept falling off the cliff, a sense of urgency developed. Detractors argued that it wasn't the fall that hurt, but the stopping. They felt fine about treating the consequences rather than the cause, but finally, wiser voices were heeded. A fence was built. The resources of the village were more wisely spent on prevention than on treating results. Giving wisely means that we give where it will do the most good—which often results in bringing blessing out of adversity.

Give Dangerously
Jesus' response to Mary's generosity was to return the favor by giving dangerously. He did so by challenging Judas, who disparaged

Mary's gift with the words, "Why the waste? This ointment could have been sold and the money used to feed the poor" (John 12:5).

Jesus would have none of that kind of disrespect: "Leave her alone," He replied. "She has done a good thing for Me, anointing My body for burial."

By challenging Judas in this way, Jesus did something quite dangerous. Judas, pained by this public censure, now had motivation to betray Jesus. *If He's talking about His death and burial,* Judas may have thought, *perhaps I can arrange it.* Jesus had to know the consequence of His rebuke; but Mary deserved our Lord's best, and He would give her nothing less. He gave dangerously.

Giving dangerously means that we count the cost but aren't cowed by the consequences. Giving dangerously means we do the right thing, even if it costs us dearly.

AN ACTION PLAN TO HELP YOU GAIN BY LOSING

> *Give gratefully.*

> *Give passionately.*

> *Give promptly.*

> *Give wisely.*

> *Give dangerously.*

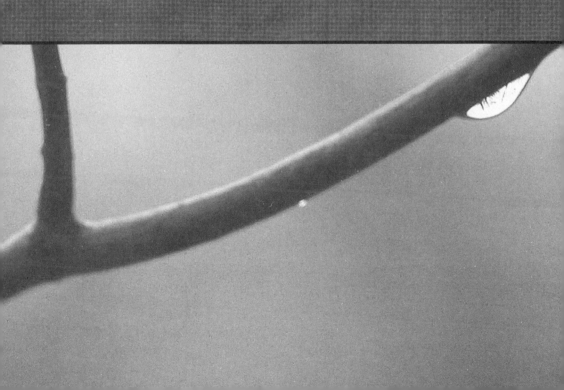

PART III:
Turning Your Adversity
into Advantage

22

SUPERSIZE YOUR FAITH

"Would you like to supersize that, sir?" It was the first time anyone had asked me this. I was clueless.

"What in the world is supersize?" I asked. I learned it was a way to get more food at so-called bargain prices. Because I didn't need the extra calories, I declined the offer, but I couldn't help thinking about the concept as I left the restaurant.

What if I could supersize life's important attributes: love, humility, faith, joy, and zeal? Wouldn't it be wonderful to simply make the request and receive an increase in the significant things of life?

Perhaps we can. Is it possible that we miss great blessings because of a faith deficit? "You have not because you ask not," admonishes James 4:2. Will we one day discover that God desired to give us bountiful blessings that we forfeited by a failure to make a simple request: "Supersize that, please"? How tragic to live a pedestrian life simply because we set our sights too low or were too lazy to ask for something more.

How desperately we need to supersize our faith. It's important because faith is such a precious and fragile commodity. We see its preciousness in the statement of Hebrews 11:6: "Without faith it is impossible to please God" (NIV). Imagine that; an attribute exists without which we can't please God. Faith is precious because "the just shall live by faith" (Romans 1:17, NKJV). But it is also fragile, perishable. Jesus, speaking of faith's short shelf life, asked an important question: "When the Son of Man comes, will he find faith on the earth?" (Luke 18:8, NIV).

In 2 Kings 13:14-22, we encounter Elisha the prophet as he approaches death. This is the man who had received a double portion of his mentor Elijah's anointing and had performed twice as many miracles as his predecessor. But now he lay dying and was visited by King Jehoash. The king was filled with great sadness, calling Elisha "father" and "the chariots and horsemen of Israel" (NIV). He was saying, in a sense, that Elisha's contribution was worth more to Israel than all its military defenses.

In the prophet's sickroom, the king wept, and Elisha sought to comfort him. He told the king to shoot an arrow out of the window. The king did. Elisha said this symbolized what God would do for Israel, giving it victory over its enemies. Elisha then asked the king to grab some more arrows and strike the ground. Jehoash complied, striking the ground three times, but the prophet seemed angry. "Why didn't you strike five or six times?" he asked the king. "If you had, God would have permitted you to totally defeat your enemies. But now, because of your halfhearted attempts, God will grant you only partial victory." The king had failed to supersize his faith.

Accept God's Plan

To supersize your faith, accept God's plan for your life. His purposes for us are better than anything we plan for ourselves, for He is omniscient—all-wise and all-knowing. He knows how long we will live and what will bring us the greatest joy. His amazing love for us can bring us to a desired destination (Jeremiah 29:11); but because we have free will, God's ideal purpose is linked to our faithfulness. He will not force us on the narrow road that leads to life (Matthew 7:13-14), though He seeks to do for us more than we can ask or imagine (Ephesians 3:20).

When Moses accepted God's plan for his life, God did more than he imagined. Moses desperately desired to enter the Promised Land, having led God's people for more than forty years through a barren wilderness. He had faithfully sought God's guidance and been, for the most part, obedient to God's commands. Then, on the border of Canaan, he made a simple request: "Lord, I want to go over into the Promised Land." And God said no.

Moses accepted God's negative response and climbed to the summit of Mount Nebo, where he eventually died. Yet we encounter this patriarch in the New Testament, standing with Elijah and Jesus on the Mount of Transfiguration (Matthew 17:3). On that mountain, Moses talked with Jesus. Though God had denied his desire to enter an earthly Promised Land, he was transported to a heavenly one, with a far more glorious future than he had imagined. It is best to accept God's plans for our lives.

How well I remember running from the ministry. Though I felt God's call on my life, I didn't want to be poor, and all the preachers I knew cultivated relationships with poverty. So I repeatedly said no to God. "Lord, choose someone else," I said. When I finally decided to do God's will, I discovered that He will not withhold good things from those who seek to serve Him (Psalm 84:11). My decision to follow His bidding has been the wisest of my life.

We see in Elisha's life his acceptance of God's plan. Although he had received a double anointing of God's Spirit, he became terminally ill (2 Kings 13) and would not be taken to heaven before death like Elijah had been. But it didn't seem to bother him, for he had learned to accept God's plan and to honor heaven's wisdom. This wisdom is rooted in accepting God's providence, so Elisha didn't complain to King Jehoash during the monarch's visit to his bedside. The king wept, but Elisha believed his life's seasons were decided by God, and he resolved to trust heaven, even when he didn't fully understand God's purposes.

Are you willing to accept God's plan for your life? If you are, take your example from Jesus, who willingly submitted to His Father's will. In the garden of Gethsemane, as the evening shadows fell, He felt the world's weight on His back and the sins of our planet suffocating His spirit, yet He resigned Himself to His Father's purposes.

He didn't *want* to die, which was why He prayed, "Father, if it is possible, let this cup pass from Me" (Matthew 26:39, NKJV). Fortunately for us, though, He added, "Nevertheless, not as I will, but as You will."

Was it not Jesus who taught His disciples to pray, "Your kingdom come, your will be done on earth as it is in heaven" (Matthew 6:10, NIV)? He permitted nothing to keep Him from accepting God's plan—not nails, ridicule, scorn, anguish, or abuse. He drank the bitter cup.

Acceptance of God's plan may force us to drink a bitter cup. It might lead to the way of the Cross, taking us through Gethsemane to Calvary to a tomb. But, like Elisha, we should feel certain that God makes no mistakes. His plans are flawless, His purposes sure. Knowing this can empower us to pray the perfect prayer: "Your will be done."

We should pray this surrender prayer because through it the tomb of despair often leads to the resurrection of possibilities. The

Father will not permit evil to triumph, and He stands within the shadows keeping watch over His children. He will not permit the devil to snatch us from His hand. In everything, He works "for the good of those who love Him and are called according to His purposes" (Romans 8:28).

A man watched a beautiful butterfly trying to emerge from a cocoon. Thinking he would help as he watched the transformation taking place, he took his penknife and slit the side of the silk cocoon. To his dismay, the butterfly flopped out of the cocoon, fell over, and lay on the ground, feebly beating its wings a few times before it died. God had a plan for that butterfly that involved struggling to emerge from the cocoon—all the pushing and wriggling was designed to develop circulation in its wings. The struggle was what prepared the butterfly for flight.

God wants to prepare you and me for flight; but without a struggle we may never get off the ground.

Respect the Sacred

Our acceptance of God's plans often derives from our respect for the sacred. King Jehoash recognized that Elisha's presence in Israel provided the nation with a defense. His concern about what the nation would endure without the prophet's wisdom showed an awareness of the sacred and an understanding that no nation flourishes without divine assistance.

Respect for the sacred is an important part of the lives of those who supersize their faith. It was a respect that was sadly missing from the lives of the young men who taunted Elisha at the beginning of his ministry. After his mentor and friend, Elijah, was taken to heaven in a fiery chariot, a group of young people—apparently aware of this miracle—shouted at Elisha, "Go up, you baldhead! Go up!" (2 Kings 2:23-24, NKJV). This was a tragic mistake, for in Elisha's defense, bears came from the woods and devoured the irreverent youth. In short, reverence and respect for sacred things may save your life.

One indication of reverence is that a person seeks to avoid premeditated sin. When sin has a logistical component, it is particularly offensive to God. David knew this and prayed, "Deliver Your servant from willful, presumptuous sins" (Psalm 19:13). Such a petition shows a certain reverential awe—the kind of attitude that those who supersize their faith will possess.

Obey Promptly

King Jehoash understood that delayed obedience is disobedience, and he did not allow himself to be guilty of such misconduct. When Elisha asked him to shoot an arrow through the window, he immediately complied (2 Kings 13:17).

Faith and obedience go together (James 2:26). In fact, one proof of faith is a willingness to act promptly. If I walked into a room and shouted "Fire!" your reaction to that cry would indicate your level of belief in my warning. If you ran from the room, I could reasonably assume that you believed me. But if you continued to do what you were doing before my warning, it would be compelling proof that you doubted the truth of my speech.

While pastoring in South Carolina, I preached a sermon one Sunday after which a young man responded to my invitation to accept Jesus as his Savior. During a potluck dinner that followed the service, he said, "Preacher, I have so much baggage in my life that I almost didn't come to Christ today. But something made me feel that this may be my last chance to get my life together." He came to the Savior just in time.

The five foolish women in Matthew 25 serve as an excellent example of delayed obedience. By waiting until the eleventh hour to purchase oil for their lamps, they were busy shopping when the bridegroom came and missed their opportunity to participate in the wedding. The five wise women had purchased their oil in advance. Their supersized faith helped them to obey promptly.

Don't Hinder God's Purpose
After telling King Jehoash to shoot the first arrow and explaining its significance, Elisha told him to strike the ground with several more arrows from his quiver. The king again obeyed promptly, but this time with limited faith. Instead of striking the ground until instructed to stop, the king gave a tepid response, striking only three times. Elisha became angry. "Why did you strike only three times? Now you will have only a partial victory" (2 Kings 13:17-19). The king's limited faith hindered what God had intended to do.

Strange as it may seem, it is possible for us to hinder God's purposes. We see this in Mark 6:5-6, when Jesus visits His hometown and His ability to do miracles is curtailed by His friends and acquaintances' lack of belief in Him. "Isn't this the carpenter's son?" they said. Because of their unbelief, Jesus couldn't do many mighty works in Nazareth.

Though some blessings come to us whether we ask for them or not, others will not come without a request. God sends His rain on the just and the unjust (Matthew 5:45), but if you don't ask for certain blessings, you won't receive them (James 4:2). James 1:5 tells us that God will give wisdom to anyone who asks in faith. And Luke 11:13 reminds us that God is eager to give His Holy Spirit to those who request Him. God made us as free moral agents, able to voluntarily serve or reject Him. He will not force His purposes on unwilling humanity. God wants more than robots; this is why Jesus couldn't do many mighty works among the people who refused to believe in Him. They hindered God.

In Matthew 16, the disciple Peter hinders Jesus. When Jesus speaks of His impending death, Peter protests and says, "This must never happen to You, Lord!" (verse 22). But it needed to happen, for Calvary's cross saved our world. Peter's lack of spiritual discernment temporarily hindered the work of God in his own life and led him to deny Christ three times.

Go the Extra Mile

Do you deliver more than is expected? Rebekah did. Her supersized faith enabled her to become Isaac's wife. In Genesis 24, Abraham's servant Eliezer sought God's guidance in finding a wife for his master's son. He asked God to lead him to someone who possessed a vigorous work ethic, who would offer to give him a drink of water and provide for his camels, as well. Rebekah came to the well and made that very offer to Eliezer. It meant hauling a significant amount of water, perhaps more than 100 gallons, but she did it, and God honored her faith. We can find blessing in adversity by going the extra mile.

AN ACTION PLAN TO HELP YOU SUPERSIZE YOUR FAITH

> *Accept God's plan.*

> *Respect the sacred.*

> *Obey promptly.*

> *Don't hinder God's purpose.*

> *Go the extra mile.*

23

BUILD A STORM-PROOF LIFE

"STAY AWAY FROM ME, CHAPLAIN," the senator said. I looked closely and saw no evidence he was kidding. With a serious countenance, he repeated himself: "Chaplain, you really should stay away."

Because this lawmaker regularly attended my weekly Bible study, I felt compelled to find the root of the problem. I asked, "Have I done something to offend you?"

"It's not you, Chaplain; it's God! He's out to get me, and I don't want to see you hurt too."

"You're serious, aren't you?"

"Yes, Chaplain, I most certainly am."

His seriousness reflected his encounter with catastrophic losses. Hurricanes Katrina and Rita had obliterated his two homes. Also, when his mother had been relocated to escape one of the storms, she had died. Having experienced such calamities, this senator felt justifiable paranoia.

Was he jinxed? Was God really out to get him? As the months

passed, he and I concluded that storms come to the just and the unjust, making it critical to build a storm-proof life.

How do we storm-proof our lives? In Matthew 7:24-27, Jesus tells us how. He says that those who hear His words and do them will build on a foundation of rock that will survive storms. He also makes it clear that storms come to all, regardless of preparation. But those who build correctly will ultimately succeed.

Remember You're Not Alone

When the prophet Elijah faced life's storms, he felt alone. "I alone am left serving You," he said to God (1 Kings 19:14). This was distorted thinking that led him to desire death, and he begged God to take his life.

To build a storm-proof life, we must avoid Elijah's distorted thinking. We must cling to the promise that God never forsakes His children (Hebrews 13:5) and that He promises to be with us even until the world ends (Matthew 28:20).

God revealed to Elijah that seven thousand others had not dishonored God. Elijah had been so preoccupied with his own personal challenges that he failed to see the fidelity of seven thousand additional disciples.

He should have known better. Thunderstorms don't discriminate. They hit the just and the unjust, the rich and the poor, the free and the incarcerated. Similarly, life's storms affect everyone. Into each life some rain must fall.

Learn to Listen to God

Part of storm-proofing our lives is hearing God's voice. Sometimes He speaks through nature, for the heavens declare His glory (Psalm 19:1). I have heard Him speak to me by a tranquil lake or on a stately mountain. His voice has whispered to me from the starry heavens. But more often than not, He speaks through His sacred Scriptures. To call the Bible the Word of God is not just a metaphor. The psalmist described it like this: "Your word is a lamp to my feet and a light for my path" (Psalm 119:105, NIV).

How clearly do you hear God's voice?

In 1 Samuel 3, Samuel hears God's voice but doesn't recognize it. When he repeatedly runs to Eli, the priest eventually instructs him to respond directly to God by saying, "Speak, Lord, for Your servant is listening." Too often, we reverse this response by crying, "Listen, Lord, for Your servant is speaking."

Peter may have done more speaking than listening, as well. In Mark 14:30, after Peter has declared his willingness to die for Christ, Jesus predicts that Peter will betray Him: "Before the rooster crows twice, you will deny Me three times."

If Peter had been really listening, he would have heard the rooster's first crowing and sought Jesus' forgiveness. But he wasn't listening, having become so spiritually deaf that he missed the first crow. He didn't even hear the God-sent alarm.

I remember a time when I had planned to sin but heard a God-sent warning. I was leaving my room to arrange my transgression when I glanced at the digital clock. It shouted 3:16 p.m. I feel certain this was providential, an instance of God's speaking to me, because I immediately thought about John 3:16. Those thoughts about God's amazing love and generosity were sufficient to keep me from evil.

Are you hearing God's voice? You must if you wish to build a storm-proof life.

Act on Your Beliefs

Jesus suggested that the storm-proof life is constructed by listening to His Word and doing it. Our rhetoric must be backed by actions. Like Paul and Silas, who sang in prison (Acts 16:25), we must develop a toughness that enables us to ride out life's storms with faithful obedience.

When one of my friends was not selected for promotion, I called to cheer him up during his season of disappointment, only to find him upbeat and optimistic. "Barry," he said, "not everybody could get promoted. Somebody had to be passed over, so why not me?"

I felt amazement, for he had been valedictorian of his Navy Advanced Course class and had an impeccable military record. But he practiced what he preached and acted on his beliefs, greeting life's setbacks with humility and faith. He had built a storm-proof life. (The good news is that he received his promotion a few years later.)

Good things happen to those who act on their beliefs, for belief without action is ineffective. James 2:26 makes it clear: "Faith without works is dead, like the body without the spirit."

One of the proofs for Jesus' resurrection was the willingness of His followers to die for their beliefs. Liars, indeed, make poor martyrs, but these disciples went to their deaths with the joy of the Lord. Their lives matched their words. They were storm-proofed for eternity.

Brace for Life's Storms

In 1 Corinthians 16:9, the apostle Paul talks about opportunity and adversity. He writes, "A great door of opportunity has opened for service, and there are many adversaries." This statement rings with truth. How often in life opportunities come with adversity attached.

Winston Churchill discovered this fact. He skillfully used his international bully pulpit to inspire his nation and the world during World War II. His eloquence flowered during the ravages of war. Martin Luther King Jr. used his bully pulpit to break down walls of segregation and discrimination in America. But his efforts required enduring the adversity of police dogs, fire hoses, bombed churches, and bloody martyrdom.

The calm with which both Churchill and King greeted life's storms reminds us of the importance of anticipating life's difficulties. King showed this anticipation in his address at the Golden Anniversary Conference of the National Urban League in September 1960. He said, "We are ready to suffer when necessary and even risk our lives to become witnesses to the truth as we see it. I realize that this approach will mean suffering and sacrifice. It may mean going to jail. . . . It may even mean physical death. But if physical death is the price that a man must pay to free his children . . . from a permanent death of the spirit, then nothing could be more redemptive."[15] Dr. King knew that a fierce tempest would accompany his freedom struggle. It was a tempest that required him to give the last full measure of devotion to the cause.

So we should brace for life's storms. This is why the man in Jesus' parable built on rock and not sand. He made the extra effort because he anticipated rain, floods, and wind. He knew it would be easier to build on the sand, but to do so would mean being ill-prepared for potential storms. He preferred to brace himself for trouble.

Stay Vigilant

When life's storms rage, what should we do? It can be disconcerting for those who serve God to face storms, even while unbelievers deal with similar challenges. We may wonder why God doesn't keep us from hardships. At such times, perhaps it's wise to remember to anticipate and watch for storms. When Hurricane Hugo hit South Carolina, my family was forced to evacuate our home because meteorologists who had kept an eye on the storm anticipated the dangers.

Fulton Sheen, a young priest with a brilliant career ahead of him, reported feeling the power of God's Spirit as he read the words of Matthew 26:40. The passage transported Sheen to Gethsemane, where Jesus was speaking to three disciples He had just awakened: "Could you not watch with Me one hour?" Jesus' words pierced Sheen's heart.

Jesus' disciples had failed Him. As He approached Golgotha, He needed their support, for His soul was exceedingly sorrowful even unto death and a storm was on the way. They were His most intimate associates, the people on whom He had leaned throughout His ministry. "Stay with Me," He had pleaded. "I especially need your support tonight." He had then entered the inner recesses of the garden, pouring out His heart in desperate prayer: "Father, if it is possible, let this cup pass from Me. Nevertheless, not as I will, but let Your will be done." Arising from His supine position, He hurried to His disciples, only to find them asleep. Disappointed, He asked them, "Was one hour of your passionate prayer too much for Me to expect from you?"

He had expected them to watch as well as pray. These are the two pillars of victorious living. Watching without prayer borders on paranoia, but praying without watching is like driving with your eyes shut. Both pillars must stand for us to live victoriously.

Sheen was so touched by Jesus' desire for human support that he made a silent commitment. *Lord*, he prayed, *for the rest of my life, I will give You that hour. I will watch with You.* In his six decades of ministry, Sheen strove to spend a minimum of one hour each day praying in a church before a crucifix of Christ. Sheen knew the importance of keeping his spirit awake, watching and praying.

Nehemiah also seemed to know the importance of this vigilance.

In Nehemiah 4:9, he describes how he turned adversity into advantage, rebuilding Jerusalem's walls in fifty-two days. Threatened by enemies who had maligned and caricatured his efforts, Nehemiah writes: "We made prayer to God, and set a watch against them day and night."

Setting a watch is different from just watching. It carries the notion of planning and intentionality, like the watches on a military ship. For the Christian, such watching happens when we see reality through the lens of God's infallible Word. It is the kind of mental stance Elisha took in 2 Kings 6:17 when he prayed that God would open the eyes of a terrified young man. Elisha saw a reality that his protégé missed, celestial help when the situation seemed desperate. Turn adversity into advantage by seeing reality from a divine perspective, as revealed in God's Word.

If we are to keep watch, we must fight slumber. Romans 13:11 tells us to awaken out of sleep, for "our salvation is nearer than when we first believed" (NKJV). We slumber when we neglect the spiritual disciplines, failing to take time for prayer and Bible study. We slumber when we think of ourselves more highly than we should, forgetting that those who think they stand often fall (1 Corinthians 10:12).

One of the saddest verses in the Bible, Judges 16:20, reports that Samson was unaware of the moment when God departed from him. Samson had slept on the lap of one of his enemies, taking for granted the special gifts God had bestowed on his life. But Delilah was a paid traitor. She bewitched Samson until he told her his secrets. When Samson awakened and rose to defend himself, he was powerless. God had left him and didn't even say good-bye. Samson had slept when he should have been watching.

The good news is that Samson turned his adversity into advantage. He did this by repenting. After he had been captured by his enemies and forced to serve as a slave, Samson turned again to God. His hair grew back, and God eventually used him to accomplish the purpose for which he was born, delivering his people from the Philistines. Samson's life teaches us to stay awake and spiritually alert.

Defeat Temptation by Watching

Keeping watch enables us to defeat temptation. The disciples in Gethsemane succumbed to the temptation to sleep because they failed to keep watch. And Jesus, understanding their limitations, said, "Your spirit was willing, but your flesh was weak" (Matthew 26:41).

Keeping watch helps you to develop a prudence that sees danger and avoids it. Joseph demonstrated this when he refused even to go near Potiphar's wife, who sought to seduce him (Genesis 39:10). This is the erring on the side of caution suggested in the challenge issued in 1 Thessalonians 5:22: "Avoid the very appearance of evil."

Cultivate Dependability

Can God trust you? Are you reliable? God thought so much of Job that He said to Satan, "Have you considered My servant Job? There is none like him in the earth" (Job 1:8). Can God say that about you?

Keeping watch enables us to be dependable. I don't want God thinking of me as unreliable. "Barry is pretty good one out of three times, or maybe three out of five, or perhaps eight out of ten." Dependable Christians rarely deviate from the path of integrity. They come through again and again.

Matthew 24:42 challenges us: "Therefore keep watch, because you do not know on what day your Lord will come" (NIV). That's what dependability is all about. When the One to whom you're accountable scrutinizes your efforts, will He be pleased? Are you sufficiently reliable that even if He comes unexpectedly, you'll be prepared? You will be if you watch as well as pray.

Deal with Life's Cares

Building a storm-proof life involves dealing with life's trials and tribulations. Indeed, all who live godly lives will experience trials (2 Timothy 3:12). But when we permit life's cares to overwhelm us, we're headed for defeat.

At the time of this writing, the news media reported of a Nebraska boy who committed random homicides at a mall before killing himself. It seems the boy felt pushed over the edge after losing his job at McDonald's and having his girlfriend break up with him.

The cares of this life can push us to extremity. That's why it is critically important for us to pull up the thorns of life's cares by watching as we pray.

Be Faithful in the Little Things

Exodus 2:3-4 chronicles the story of Moses' sister, Miriam, who watched the small vessel on the Nile River designed to keep her brother from death. Pharaoh had decreed that the Israelites' male children should die, and Moses' parents had defied this decree, depending on their daughter's faithfulness to buy time for the baby. "Watch over him carefully," I can hear them say to Miriam. Miriam did and became God's instrument for saving her brother's life. Her faithfulness in the little things brought blessing out of adversity. The blessing became so great that Moses' mother was actually paid to rear her own son by the man who had decreed his death.

Jesus said, "Whoever can be trusted with very little can also be trusted with much" (Luke 16:10, NIV). The true test of our character is our faithfulness in the little things. When God was helping Gideon put together an army, He tested the recruits by asking them to drink water (Judges 7). As God watched how they drank, He was able to determine who would be useful for His purposes and who wouldn't. A small action, drinking water, was all God needed to make the determination. Only three hundred of ten thousand passed the test.

Number Your Days
One of the best motivations for watching is the transitory nature of life. In Psalm 90, we're admonished to "number our days." Not our years, months, or weeks. At best, we get only days. Because we never know when life will end, we should consistently watch.

Jesus said, "Keep watch because you do not know when the owner of the house will come back" (Mark 13:35, NIV). When we die, we will meet our Creator. Will we be ready? A few days ago, I held a memorial service for a handsome young man who was killed in an automobile accident at the age of twenty-five. I pointed out at the service how brief is this sojourn we call life and that some of us live summer days while others live only winter ones. Winter days are much shorter. Ecclesiastes 9:12 says that we don't know when our time will come. We're like fish caught in a trap or birds caught in a snare—trapped in an instant when we least expect it. In *Macbeth*, Shakespeare writes of our brief existence: "Out, out, brief candle!" The ephemeral nature of our earthly pilgrimage should prompt us to stay alert, to continue to watch.

Receive Inspiration from Those Who Have Gone Before
The final reason for keeping watch is the exemplary lives of those who have gone before us. Biblical heroes and heroines have left us great legacies of courage, reliability, and consistency—people

such as Esther, Daniel, Joseph, Paul, and others. The writer of Hebrews says, "We are surrounded by such a great cloud of witnesses" (Hebrews 12:1, NIV). Like Americans in the nineteenth century fighting with the battle cry "Remember the Alamo," so we should move into the future inspired by the sterling examples of others' faithful lives, determined not to settle for less than excellence. This is a sure path toward finding blessing in adversity.

AN ACTION PLAN TO HELP YOU BUILD A STORM-PROOF LIFE

> *Remember you're not alone.*

> *Learn to listen to God.*

> *Act on your beliefs.*

> *Brace for life's storms.*

> *Stay vigilant.*

> *Defeat temptation by watching.*

> *Cultivate dependability.*

> *Deal with life's cares.*

> *Be faithful in the little things.*

> *Number your days.*

> *Receive inspiration from those who have gone before.*

A Final Word

I READ ONCE ABOUT A YOUNG CHRISTIAN who invested his life's savings in a peach orchard. He worked diligently, pruning the trees and removing the weeds, preparing for a bumper crop of peaches. In the spring, the orchard blossomed beautifully and the fruit set well. But then a frost came and destroyed the entire crop. The man became upset with God and quit going to church.

After he had missed the worship service for several weeks, his pastor paid him a visit.

"I've missed seeing you in church, Bob," the pastor said.

"I'm not coming to church anymore, Pastor," Bob responded. "Do you think I can worship a God who cares so little for me that He would let a frost kill all my peaches?"

The pastor replied calmly and wisely, "Son, God loves you better than He loves your peaches. You see, God understands that though peaches can grow without frost, believers can't grow without trials. God isn't in the business of growing peaches. He's in the business of growing believers and making them strong."

When trouble comes, look for God's blessing in your adversity. He is in the business of growing believers who can withstand life's storms.

Notes

1. Eleanor Roosevelt, *It Seems to Me* (New York: Norton, 1954).
2. C. S. Lewis, letter to Father Peter Bide, April 29, 1959, in *Letters of C. S. Lewis*, Walter Hooper, ed. (Orlando, FL: Harcourt, 1993), 477.
3. http://investing-school.com/history/52-must-read-quotes-from-legendary-investor-warren-buffett.
4. James Russell Lowell, "The Present Crisis," *Yale Book of American Verse*, Thomas R. Lounsbury, ed. (New Haven: Yale University, 1912), 128.
5. Martin Luther King Jr., "Three Dimensions of a Complete Life," a sermon first preached at Dexter Avenue Baptist Church, Birmingham, Alabama, in 1954.
6. Fulton J. Sheen, *Life Is Worth Living* (San Francisco: Ignatius Press, 1953), 193–194.
7. H. R. Palmer, "Yield Not to Temptation" (1868).
8. William Shakespeare, *As You Like It*, act 2, scene 1, lines 12–17.
9. James Allen Francis, "One Solitary Life," Palmer G. Brown, ed. (Glendale, CA: Karen Brown Agency, 1973).
10. Guy Berryman, Jonny Buckland, Will Champion, and Chris Martin, "Viva La Vida" (Universal Music Publishing, 2008).
11. John Wooden and Steve Jamison, *The Essential Wooden: A Lifetime of Lessons on Leaders and Leadership* (New York: McGraw Hill, 2007), xi.
12. Ibid., 33.
13. Augustine, *Confessions*, trans. Henry Chadwick (New York: Oxford University Press, 1991), 3.
14. Ira Stanphill, "I Know Who Holds Tomorrow" (New Spring, 1950).
15. Martin Luther King Jr., *The Papers of Martin Luther King Jr.*, vol. 5, Clayborne Carson, ed. (Berkeley: University of California Press, 2005), 504–505.

About the Author

ON JUNE 27, 2003, Rear Admiral Barry C. Black (Ret.) was elected the 62nd chaplain of the United States Senate, an office first established in 1789. Prior to coming to Capitol Hill, Chaplain Black served in the U.S. Navy for more than twenty-seven years, ending his distinguished career as the chief of Navy chaplains.

Commissioned as a Navy chaplain in 1976, Chaplain Black's first duty station was the Fleet Religious Support Activity in Norfolk, Virginia. Subsequent assignments included Naval Support Activity, Philadelphia, Pennsylvania; U.S. Naval Academy, Annapolis, Maryland; First Marine Aircraft Wing, Okinawa, Japan; Naval Training Center, San Diego, California; USS *Belleau Wood* (LHA 3), Long Beach, California; Naval Chaplains School Advanced Course, Newport, Rhode Island; Marine Aircraft Group 31, Beaufort, South Carolina; Assistant Staff Chaplain, Chief of Naval Education and Training, Pensacola, Florida; and Fleet Chaplain, U.S. Atlantic Fleet, Norfolk, Virginia.

As rear admiral, his personal decorations included the Navy Distinguished Service Medal, the Legion of Merit Medal, Defense Meritorious Service Medal (two medals), Meritorious Service Medals (two awards), Navy and Marine Corps Commendation

Medals (two awards), and numerous unit awards, campaign, and service medals.

Chaplain Black is a native of Baltimore, Maryland, and an alumnus of Oakwood College, Andrews University, North Carolina Central University, Eastern Baptist Seminary, Salve Regina University, and United States International University. In addition to earning master of arts degrees in divinity, counseling, and management, he has received a doctoral degree in ministry and a doctor of philosophy degree in psychology.

Chaplain Black has been recognized for many outstanding achievements. Of particular note, he was chosen from 127 nominees for the 1995 NAACP Renowned Service Award for his contribution to equal opportunity and civil rights. He also received the 2002 Benjamin Elijah Mays Distinguished Leadership Award from the Morehouse School of Religion. In 2004, the Old Dominion University chapter of the NAACP conferred on him the Image Award, "Reaffirming the Dream—Realizing the Vision," for military excellence.

Chaplain Black is married to the former Brenda Pearsall of St. Petersburg, Florida. They have three sons: Barry II, Brendan, and Bradford.